Navigating the First Years

Navigating the First Years

A Toolkit for Classroom Success

Vince Bustamante

Sarah Adomako-Ansah

Tim Cusack

Wayne Davies

Foreword by Marcia L. Tate

CORWIN

For information:

Corwin
A Sage Company
2455 Teller Road
Thousand Oaks, California 91320
(800) 233-9936
www.corwin.com

Sage Publications Ltd.
1 Oliver's Yard
55 City Road
London, EC1Y 1SP
United Kingdom

Sage Publications India Pvt. Ltd.
Unit No 323-333, Third Floor, F-Block
International Trade Tower Nehru Place
New Delhi 110 019
India

Sage Publications Asia-Pacific Pte. Ltd.
18 Cross Street #10-10/11/12
China Square Central
Singapore 048423

Vice President and Editorial Director: Monica Eckman
Senior Publisher: Jessica Allan
Senior Content Development Editor: Mia Rodriguez
Senior Editorial Assistant: Natalie Delpino
Production Editor: Vijayakumar
Copy Editor: Diane DiMura
Typesetter: TNQ Tech Pvt. Ltd.
Proofreader: Girish Sharma
Indexer: TNQ Tech Pvt. Ltd.
Cover Designer: Gail Buschman
Marketing Manager: Olivia Bartlett

Printed and bound by CPI Group (UK) Ltd, Croydon, CR0 4YY

ISBN 978-1-0719-7362-2

This book is printed on acid-free paper.

25 26 27 28 29 10 9 8 7 6 5 4 3 2 1

CONTENTS

Note From the Publisher: The authors have provided a link in this book available to you through QR (quick response) code. To read a QR code, you must have a smartphone or tablet with a camera. We recommend that you download a QR code reader app that is made specifically for your phone or tablet brand.

FOREWORD

NAVIGATING THE FIRST YEARS

We truly belong to a sacred society! We are educators and are part of the only profession that impacts every other profession! Every doctor, lawyer, electrician, or cosmetologist comes by way of a teacher; therefore, it would behoove us to recruit and retain as many qualified prospective educators as possible.

Since the authors of this book so effectively use the strategy of storytelling to share their personal and meaningful, though diverse, experiences, I thought I would follow suit. Here is my story!

I knew that I would become a teacher when I was six years old. I used to line my dolls up in my bedroom and teach them for hours. Funny . . . I didn't have a single behavior problem! My Chatty Cathy doll would not even talk unless I pulled her string. (I realize that most beginning teachers today have no idea what a Chatty Cathy doll is.) I went on to major in education and began my career in 1974 with a major school district in Atlanta, Georgia. That would make this my fiftieth year in education and I have loved every minute of it! I started with 34 fourth graders, 20 of whom were boys, and I was mediocre at best. If I had had this resource, I am certain I would have been more successful from the very beginning.

In the Introduction, the authors delineate the positive attributes of an exceptional teacher to which we should all aspire. Then the remainder of the book addresses seven major categories, based on research, that should be an integral part of every beginning teacher's preparation program. The New Teacher Inventory is particularly effective since it enables the reader to assess those characteristics that they already possess and can build upon.

"Creating classrooms free from racism, bias, and judgment is integral to this mission" is a wonderful summary statement for chapter 1. Being a woman of color, I recognize the importance of this chapter and love the footrace analogy that enables readers to discern the difference between equality and equity.

Chapter 2 speaks solely to the numerous educators we have lost due to burnout, especially as a result of the pandemic. In my half-century of experience and over time, I have learned the importance of balancing personal and work life. Chapter 2 provides some definitive ways to do just that!

Beginning teachers can be overwhelmed with all the policies and procedures they must follow. Discussing that content in chapter 3 with a mentor can be invaluable. So can the planning in chapter 4. When that planning is collaborative, it can be far more effective. As a beginning teacher, any lesson plans I made were without the guidance of my more experienced colleagues. There was also no such thing as a mentor or coach to assist me.

The key elements of an effective learning environment are delineated in chapters 5 and 6. Classroom management is not everything, but it can make everything else possible! In fact, I have written a classroom management book that addresses those very same elements—including physical and psychological safety, emotional support, and engagement. After all, your best defense against classroom management challenges is an engaging lesson.

If you wait until you finish that lesson to assess it, you have waited too late! Chapter 7 provides both formative and summative tools for determining if students are truly learning.

You are about to embark on a wonderful journey! Four master educators share their personal stories and those of others to equip you with the tools I did not have 50 years ago when I began my career. Did I eventually become a good teacher? Yes, I did! But why not begin changing the lives of students from day one by adding *Navigating the First Years* to your professional library? It will certainly be in mine so that I can share this crucial information with everyone who needs it. And everyone needs it!

Dr. Marcia L. Tate

ACKNOWLEDGMENTS

From Vince Bustamante:

The conceptualization and creation of this project would not have been possible without the guidance, conversation, and perspectives of many wonderful people. I am grateful to my coauthors, Sarah, Wayne, and Tim for their skills, diverse perspectives, and unique abilities as they lent their voices to this project. Individually you are all such talented individuals, but collectively we became even stronger. Thank you for joining me on this journey.

A big thank you to everyone at Corwin who supported this project, and helped make this a reality. A special thank you to Monica Eckman for seeing the value in this project, and in me as an author. Without your support, this book would cease to exist. Also thank you to Jessica Allan, and your editorial team for your guidance throughout the writing process. I am so excited for our future projects together. Finally, I express my sincerest gratitude to Dr. Marcia Tate for writing a wonderful foreword for this book. Your work has been inspiring to me as an educator and to have you write this for us is truly a dream come true.

This book has been a labor of love and a long-held dream of mine. My commitment to supporting new teachers stems from a desire to ensure they are equipped with the right tools and preparation to thrive in their roles. I believe that adequate support and preparation are essential for cultivating the next generation of exceptional educators. I am truly grateful that this project can serve as a valuable resource in the new teacher toolkit.

Finally, and most importantly thank you to my family. Leah you are a source of support, guidance, perspective, and unconditional love. Thank you for believing in me and for being the foundation of our household, without you none of this is possible. Luca, thank you for giving me the greatest job I could ever ask for, being your dad. I am so excited for you to become a big brother.

From Sarah Adomako-Ansah:

Writing this book has been an incredible journey, not just in terms of research and collaboration, but also as a personal voyage of self-discovery. Throughout this process, I've learned so much about myself—about my resilience, my perspectives, and my capacity for growth. This endeavor has been as much about introspection as it has been about sharing insights with others.

First and foremost, I extend my deepest gratitude to my coauthors, Vince Bustamante, Tim Cusack, and Wayne Davies. Your patience, expertise, dedication, and passion have made this collaboration a truly enriching experience. Thank you for your invaluable insights and commitment to bringing this project to life.

To my parents, Anthony and Elizabeth, thank you for being my first teachers and for instilling in me a love of learning. Your unwavering support and encouragement have been the foundation of my journey, and I am forever grateful for your guidance. Thanks as well, to my siblings Daniel and Samantha, as well as to David, who guides me every step of the way.

A special thanks to the incredible team at Corwin. Your professionalism, dedication, and belief in our work have been instrumental in bringing this book to fruition. Your hard work behind the scenes does not go unnoticed, and we are deeply appreciative of your efforts.

Finally, thank you to the reader for engaging with this work. I hope that this vocation you have chosen is one you truly are passionate about and see longevity in. Here's to education!

From Wayne Davies:

As I reflect on all that has gone into the writing of this book, I want to thank my coauthors, Vince, Sara, and Tim who I am forever grateful to have spent time getting to know and write with, over the past several months and years. You are each wonderfully talented educators who bring vastly, yet complimentary knowledge and experiences to the writing table. Your passion and concern for ensuring emerging teachers are well-resourced and supported is commendable. I look forward to more evening spent on online platforms talking about educational issues with you!

I would be remiss if I did not thank Tess, Kendall, and Clyde for being the reason that I look forward to getting home after every trip. You are the best part of my world. Your patience with all the nights I spend writing, days that I am away, and times that I am lost in thought, is appreciated more than you will ever know. Kendall and Clyde—your journeys are just beginning and I know you will be great at whatever you choose to do.

Much of this writing was shaped by my years as a teacher and school and district leader. I was blessed to work with incredibly talented staff and students who pushed me to be better and at other times simply assured me I was on the right track. There was also many caregivers and parents that I sat with who truly loved their kids and while there were occasional bumps, always came back to the table to talk about what was best for their children. It is these people, I would encourage teachers to listen to, ask questions of, and then act in the best interests of.

My perspective is also shaped by being a citizen of the Red River Metis Nation who have shown me nothing but unwavering support in my educational pursuits. You have consistently proven that support of education is what will make this world a more just and fairer place for all people, especially those who are Indigenous. Your support has led to this and other projects I am able to contribute toward. I hope I have done you proud and can continue to give back.

To the Corwin family, thank you for your support in writing this book as well as becoming a member of your team, facilitating professional learning in school districts in a variety of locations. Your collegiality and enduring ability to give me the tools and motivation I need, has made a true difference. I am loathe to "name names" as I could fill up this page and still miss someone. Suffice it to say, you know who you are and you have made my life personally and professionally better.

To Marion the librarian, Gayle and Billy Bedard, and the Hughes family and all the other people who helped me thrive and survive during my beginning years of teaching at Lax Kw'alaams and in Prince Rupert, thank you. Your love, support, and patience helped me grab a toehold in a career I have loved and that has given me so much. It is within that spirit that I also acknowledge every emerging teacher who is reading this book, whether you are entering your very first career or you are a person who made a career change or an internationally trained teacher making a location change, that we believe in you! I hope this book resonates with you and provides you with information and ideas that contribute to your success.

From Tim Cusack:

I begin with an expression of deep gratitude for my talented colleagues Sarah, Vince, and Wayne for the passion and experience they bring to teacher development. Writing this book with them has been a rich learning experience and meaningful opportunity to contribute to the important work of preparing our early career teachers. As a former school superintendent who went back to university to serve as a dean of education, I am ever mindful of the importance of equipping new teachers to not merely survive those first formative years of teaching but to learn key skills and gain the confidence needed to thrive!

My 30+ years of classroom teaching, school and system leadership reminds me that there is no greater investment than in the education of our children. With my own children now entering the profession, I realize that change and challenge is inevitable in being a teacher today. It is how we equip our new teachers to engage with what their 30+ years brings, that compels me to champion all early career teachers in the hope that they will flourish as educators and remain engaged in the teaching and learning of children. Thus, I am so thankful for this book and the ideas shared by this team of authors.

To the amazing and supportive staff at Corwin Press, thank you! From book pitch to publication, the passion of the Corwin team is evident in each step of the process. Your advocacy for great teaching and learning is inspiring and I am humble to serve as an author and consultant in sharing this important work.

Finally, I wish to thank my wife, Susan, for her ongoing support and perspectives on great teaching and leading. As well, I thank my sons, Patrick, Nicolas, and Ian for enkindling in me my "why" for teaching. You remind me that I too, as a student of lifelong learning, have much still to learn from each of you. My wish is that this book will help you and all who serve the noble profession of teaching (in its many forms) to flourish and thrive.

PUBLISHER'S ACKNOWLEDGMENTS

Corwin gratefully acknowledges the contributions of the following reviewer:

Serena Pariser
Author and Teacher, Yinghua Charter School
Minneapolis, Minnesota

ABOUT THE AUTHORS

Vince Bustamante, Ed.D., is a Calgary-based instructional coach, curriculum content developer, and author. Vince specializes in working with teachers, leadership teams, schools, and school districts in implementing high impact strategies and systems. With a strong background in implementation, assessment, and deep learning, he is passionate about understanding and evaluating teachers' impact. Having worked with schools and school districts across North America and internationally, he brings a wide variety of experience and perspectives when looking at school improvement, pedagogical and leadership development, and implementation of high impact strategies across school environments. Vince's doctoral research focused on the sustainable implementation of professional learning across school districts and the impact of long-term school partnerships.

Vince has co-authored two bestselling books with Corwin Press: *Great Teaching by Design* and *The Assessment Playbook for Distance and Blended Learning*. His other title: *Leader Ready: Four Pathways to Prepare Aspiring School Leaders* is also available from Corwin Press. You can find more information about Vince at: www.vincebustamante.com.

Sarah Adomako-Ansah is a graduate of the University of Alberta, B Ed (2013). She is a former teacher with the Edmonton Catholic School Division, teaching Grades 3 through 6 from 2013 until 2021. She was the Division's first Equity, Diversity, Inclusion, and Anti-Racism Consultant in 2023 and provided support to administration, teachers, and students in their journey with this important topic. In 2021, she began her term as the Educator in Residence at the Canadian Museum for Human Rights, supporting human rights education in Canada, but also creating a program titled "Pass the Mic: Let's Talk About Racism." Currently, she has left the classroom and is now the Manager, Education Outreach for the CMHR. In addition, Sarah is the cofounder of the Black Teacher's Association of Alberta and strives to amplify all voices in schools. Finally, she is the fortunate recipient of both the Queen Elizabeth II Platinum Jubilee Medal and the Randy Palivoda Award for her efforts in contributing to human rights and diversity in education and leadership.

Wayne Davies, Ed.D., is the Director of Student Teaching at the University of Winnipeg where he also teaches. Prior to this role, he spent 32 years as a teacher and school leader. He has taught and led in many settings including on the Lax Kw'alaams reserve in British Columbia, Canada as well as in rural and urban school divisions in Manitoba. As a principal in Selkirk, Wayne was part of the nationally acclaimed BOSS Guitar Works project which he eventually wrote about in his novel "The Guitar Principal." In 2014, Wayne was recognized as one of Canada's top 40 school leaders and is a Distinguished Alumnus at the University of Manitoba for his community work. A citizen of the Red River Métis, Wayne holds an Ed.D in educational leadership from the University of Western Ontario where his work focused on high school graduation rates and the role of culture, student voice, and two-eyed seeing in increasing Indigenous student success.

Timothy P. Cusack, Ed.D, has over 32 years of experience as a classroom teacher, assistant principal, principal, and superintendent. Having taught in rural boards in northern and southern Alberta, Tim also has ten years of experience as school leader (K–12) and eight years of experience as a system leader of a large urban board of over 48,000 students in Edmonton. Tim now serves as the Dean of Education of Concordia University of Edmonton (CUE) where he leads a teacher preparation program (After Degree in Education) and a Master of Education in Educational Leadership program. His doctoral research focuses on new teacher preparation, teacher mentorship, and leadership development. His dissertation (University of Portland 2020), which centered on preparing aspiring school leaders, evolved into his first book with Corwin: *Leader Ready: Four Pathways to Prepare Aspiring School Leaders* (2023).

Tim has worked with school jurisdictions across Canada and the United States in sharing his passion for leadership development and teacher mentorship. He is well known for his commitment to public education and school system improvement. His service to public education has been recognized through the Council of School Leadership Distinguished Leadership Award (2014), The Queen Elizabeth II Platinum Jubilee Medal (2023).

Tim also serves as a Naval Warfare Officer in the Royal Canadian Navy and brings a wealth of leadership experience having served now for over 35 years including tours as both an Executive and Commanding Officer. In addition to his role of Dean at (CUE), Tim is currently the Commanding Officer of HMCS NONSUCH, Edmonton's Naval Reserve Division. His experience in K–12 education, post-secondary leadership, and military leadership adds richness and depth to his work as an educational consultant and author.

More information about Tim may be found at: www.timothycusack.com

INTRODUCTION

YOU ARE HERE, AND HERE IS WHERE YOU ARE SUPPOSED TO BE!

If you are reading this you must be a new teacher, an aspiring teacher, or someone who knows a new teacher. Regardless of how you found your way to this book, welcome and thank you for your dedication to one of the most rewarding careers on the planet!

> As you step into your role as a teacher, know that you are embarking on a profound and transformative journey—one that will shape not only the minds of young learners but also the very fabric of our society.

You are so important! Teaching is a noble and profound profession, and one that is not for everyone. But by choosing to embark on this journey you have chosen to selflessly impact many lives in a variety of different ways.

Allow us to illuminate this truth:

1. The Architects of Dreams: You hold the blueprint for dreams. Within your classroom walls, seeds of curiosity, creativity, and resilience are sown. You are the architect who designs the

foundation upon which future doctors, artists, engineers, and leaders will build their aspirations.

2. The Compassionate Guides: As a teacher, you are more than a dispenser of knowledge. You are a beacon of empathy, compassion, and understanding. Your words and actions have the power to heal wounds, ignite passions, and instill confidence. You guide students through storms, celebrating their victories and wiping away their tears.
3. The Weavers of Community: In your classroom, diversity converges. You weave a tapestry of cultures, languages, and experiences. You create a safe haven where differences are celebrated, where every child feels seen and valued. You foster connections that transcend textbooks—a community that thrives on kindness and respect.
4. The Keepers of Hope: When the world feels uncertain, you are the steady hand that holds hope. You believe in the potential of every child, even when they doubt themselves. Your unwavering commitment fuels the flame of possibility, reminding us all that education is the key to a brighter future.
5. The Innovators and Lifelong Learners: Teaching is not static; it's an ever-evolving dance. You adapt, experiment, and refine. You embrace technology, pedagogical shifts, and fresh ideas. You model lifelong learning, showing your students that growth knows no bounds.
6. The Ripple Effect: Your impact extends beyond the classroom. Each lesson you teach, each smile you share, creates ripples that reach families, communities, and generations. You are part of an intricate web of change, and your influence is immeasurable.

So, as you embark on this noble voyage, remember that you are not alone. You stand shoulder to shoulder with a community of passionate educators who believe in the power of learning. Your dedication will shape the world, one student at a time.

WHY THIS BOOK IS IMPORTANT TO US?

We know there are plenty of books out there intended for new teachers and we also are very aware that we are not new teachers anymore, however; all of us in our own capacity have an affinity for supporting new and beginning teachers. After all, we were all in the same place you are now and in many ways our stories and our whys are what led us to collaborate on this project that we are all passionate about. While we all have navigated through the tumultuous first years, we are now in different places in our careers to offer our perspectives and ideas to help make your transition into this career as smooth as possible. Here are some of the reasons we decided to collaborate on this text.

Vince Bustamante, Currently a Best-Selling Author, Consultant, and a Former Middle and High School Teacher

I vividly remember my first few days at my school, you see I joined the staff halfway through their school year and was put in a position where I had a few short weeks to get the students ready for their semester final exams. I remember the exciting feeling of having my own classroom as I met with the leadership team for the first time. I quickly realized that I accepted a position that was extremely complicated, and I was going to have to put in long hours just to get my students caught up. I had very little interaction with other staff members, and it was very difficult coming into a school midyear and having to learn about the school culture all while simultaneously trying to navigate a complex teaching schedule. Needless to say, I was spending 12 to 14 hours a day, 6 days a week (I always took Saturdays off) just trying to keep up.

A HUGE wakeup call happened during my fourth week in the role . . . after spending 13 hours at school on a Wednesday (after having 12+ hour days on Monday and Tuesday) I was tired and decided to head home. On the way home, I hit a patch of black ice and slammed into oncoming traffic. My car was totaled and somehow, I escaped with no injuries, but I was very shaken up. It was that evening and over the next few days I realized that to survive as a new teacher I needed to reach out for support. So, the next day, I went into school and had a meeting with my assistant principal. The leadership team subsequently provided the support I needed and continued to do so over my first year.

The moral of the story is it took a car accident for me to realize that I needed to advocate for myself. I made a promise to myself that as I continued to teach that I would always advocate for the support of new teachers and I myself would share as much knowledge as possible to make sure the new teachers I encounter always feel supported and valued.

Sarah Adomako-Ansah, Currently the Manager of Educational Outreach at the Canadian Museum for Human Rights

Teaching has always been a vocation I felt drawn to. I come from a large family with many educators. I remember being a child, learning math at the kitchen table with my father, a teacher as well, by way of Ghana, located in West Africa. His gentle approach in teaching me concepts in a subject that I was not confident in helped me see that teaching is something I could do. I was also lucky enough to have many of my elementary teachers tap me on the shoulder to tell me, "You'd be great at this." In moments where I considered a different career, education always reappeared to remind me of the impact I could have on students.

Growing up, I had a twin brother. Sadly, he passed in June of 2013, but graduated from postsecondary a month prior to his untimely death. We discussed so many things and shared many of the same sentiments, but one that sticks out to me constantly is our shared wish for representation in our schools growing up and in our respective fields as young adults. Neither of us had a Black educator through our K–12 education experience or in postsecondary. It would have made our experiences even more memorable.

I was privileged to be the representation that I so desperately sought after in 2013. I began my career at an elementary school in a Grade 3 and 4 combined classroom and realized the importance of being a young Black woman in front of a group of 25 students, eight of whom were Black girls. The relationships built over the next eight years as a teacher at that school continued to prove to me that I was in the right place at the right time—I was called to be a teacher to be the representation that is so important in our world. Although I'm no longer a K–12 educator, after a secondment opportunity and a year as a school board consultant, my new career affords me the ability to continue the representation that I still seek as a young Black woman. I have the privilege and pleasure to lead a team of educators to support human rights education in my country. I have the ability to work with school leaders and support them, so that, in turn, they can support their staff and students. To see other people of color in leadership roles like mine is the inspiration that fuels me.

Welcome to the wild world of teaching. You're going to love it here.

Tim Cusack, Currently a Dean of Education and Former Central Office and School Leader

I recall fondly the mentor teachers and university facilitators who walked alongside me during the practical components of my bachelor of education in 1992–1993. I had three field placements over the span of my program and in each case, direct observation with feedback given, and supervision of my fledgling practice was at a high level of engagement. I had frequent debriefings and opportunities for reflection of how my lessons went. Topics such as what approaches to the lesson might I do differently next time, what aspects of the classroom dynamic I might want to improve, and receiving celebratory feedback on what worked well, were valued added to my learning preservice experience.

Once I commenced teaching the following Fall in a remote rural school in Northern Alberta, the level of support and feedback I had at university subsided to the business of school routines, supervision, extracurricular tasks, and campus life with no formal mentor (or even grade partner). This left me largely on my own to figure out how to be an effective beginning teacher. It is not that the other teachers on staff and administration weren't kind or helpful, but in the most formative years of my teaching, the art and craft of good learning and assessment, were left more to chance than intentional design. That said, in time, and with a lot of learning from trial and error, I become more capable and proficient. In time, I would move on to different schools, different districts, and roles such as department head, assistant principal, principal and central office leadership. As a lifelong learner, I never forget that I am always a teacher first!

After 31 years of service as a teacher and leader at all levels K-12 in rural, suburban, and large urban centers, I switched gears to become dean of education at Concordia University of Edmonton. In a way, I was a superintendent who wanted to go back to school. Why? To help better equip and prepare the early career teachers we so greatly need, to not simply survive those first few formative years, but to thrive and flourish. Through my research and work with mentor teachers and university facilitators, I want to help create practical and helpful resources that give all early career teachers, and the school staff who welcome them, the best chances for success and retention.

Wayne Davies, Currently a Director of Student Teaching and Former School Leader

> Stepping out of the floatplane onto the dock, I took a deep breath, smelled the sea air and looked at the mountains, all the while trying to contemplate the magnitude of the decision I had made three weeks prior. Taking your first teaching position in a community, sight unseen, over 1700 miles from your hometown, was much like realizing your roller coaster seatbelt is undone—exhilarating and terrifying all at the same time! Perhaps you experienced a few of those feelings too, as you walked into your classroom the first time.
>
> To be frank, what I didn't know about teaching was only surpassed by how little I knew about the local Tsimshian culture and history of the Lax Kw'alaams Reserve, which I was now immersed in. And while my colleagues would help me unlock what successful teaching practices looked like, it would be my students, their caregivers, and elders who would help me find success in the community. They engaged me in conversation about life on a First Nations Reserve, the history and culture of the people, and many other nuances of rural living. Their willingness to impart knowledge, paired with my desire to learn, reflect, and incorporate all I was receiving would eventually allow me to move from surviving to thriving over the coming 32 years as a teacher, school, and district leader.
>
> Now, as a director of student teaching, I see students heading out to their placements and eventually on to their first "paid gig." I know, just like all who have gone before them, that their learning curve will be steep. However, if they work hard, the rewards will be many, and over time, they will move from rookie to seasoned veteran. I tell them that the answers are out there but that they will need to work hard, self-reflect, and talk to their colleagues and community to find them. This is why I see this book as an important resource. It will be best read with other teachers of varying levels of experience. Engage them, ask them what they think or how they would handle the situations we reference, and then get them to make their thinking explicit so you can understand how they arrived at their conclusions. You may not agree with them, but at the very least you will be actively engaged in conversation and reflection, both extremely powerful tools for your development over those first days, weeks, and months. Good luck, you're gonna be great!

You see, all of us in our own right have our why. For some of us, it took a huge life event to wake us up, and others not so much but collectively we all agree that the future of our classrooms and our schools are in the hands of new and beginning teachers. We hope that over the course of reading this book, you also feel supported as you navigate through your first few years of being in the classroom. Of course it goes without saying that it is our hope that this book supports your previous or current learning that is occurring in your university courses, or through your current lived experiences (especially if you are in the classroom right now). Upon reading through this we hope you feel as prepared as possible to be the best teacher you possibly can be.

SOME RESEARCH ON TEACHER PREPAREDNESS

In today's dynamic educational landscape, the role of teachers is fundamental in shaping the learning experiences and outcomes of students.

> As educational paradigms evolve and classrooms become more diverse, the importance of equipping teachers with the proper skills cannot be overstated.

New teacher preparation stands as a cornerstone in fostering quality education and student success. Its significance lies in equipping educators with the necessary skills, knowledge, and competencies to address the diverse needs of learners and navigate the complexities of contemporary classrooms. As we looked at the research on new teacher preparation, it was clear that there are a few major categories that are imperative to success in the classroom.

PEDAGOGICAL STRATEGIES

Central to effective teaching are pedagogical strategies that cater to the diverse needs of learners. New teacher skills encompass the mastery of evidence-based instructional techniques such as differentiated instruction, inquiry-based learning, and collaborative learning approaches (Darling-Hammond, 2017). By employing varied pedagogical methods, educators create inclusive learning environments that foster student engagement, critical thinking, and academic achievement. Through a variety of research driven instructional practices, new teachers can often become successful very quickly, especially if they break away from the notion of "I teach the way I like to learn."

TECHNOLOGY INTEGRATION

Technology is no longer a tool but a way of life and as such, proficiency in technology integration is imperative for educators. New teacher skills involve leveraging digital tools, educational software, and online resources to enhance teaching and learning experiences (Williams, 2022). By integrating technology into instruction, teachers create interactive lessons, facilitate virtual collaboration, and promote digital literacy skills, preparing students for success in the digital age. It is also important for new teachers to manage the rapidly changing educational-technology landscape and learn how to manage technology as a tool for instruction and also a potential distraction for students.

SOCIAL-EMOTIONAL LEARNING (SEL)

Beyond academic achievement, nurturing students' social and emotional well-being is paramount. New teachers that encompass the ability to integrate social-emotional learning (SEL) competencies into the curriculum, fostering self-awareness, empathy, and resilience, often find greater academic success with their classes (Durlak et al., 2011). Educators equipped with SEL strategies create supportive classroom environments where students feel valued, understood, and empowered to succeed academically and personally. It is often the case that no instructional progress is made when students do not feel safe emotionally, and thus on some days socioemotional learning will trump any academic learning; and that's okay!

CULTURAL COMPETENCE

Most classrooms are beautifully diverse and as such, cultural competence is essential for effective teaching. New teachers must be understanding and appreciative of diverse cultural backgrounds, perspectives, and experiences (Gay, 2018). Culturally responsive teaching practices recognize the unique strengths and needs of each student, promoting inclusivity, equity, and academic success. All students deserve to be seen, heard, understood, and valued, period.

CRITICAL THINKING AND PROBLEM-SOLVING

In an ever-changing world, critical thinking and problem-solving skills are indispensable for students. New teachers should foster students' analytical thinking, creativity, and problem-solving abilities (Darling-Hammond, 2017). By incorporating inquiry-based learning, project-based tasks, and real-world challenges into instruction, teachers empower students to think critically, make informed decisions, and tackle complex problems effectively.

COLLABORATION AND COMMUNICATION

Effective teaching entails collaboration and communication with students, colleagues, parents, and community stakeholders. Collaboration is essential to new teacher survival in the first few years of teaching. Incorporating the ability to collaborate with peers, communicate effectively with diverse audiences, and engage parents in their children's education will in turn create opportunities to progress and grow in the classroom (Little, 1993). By fostering partnerships and building a supportive network, educators create a collaborative learning community that enhances student learning and well-being.

By no means is this list comprehensive, but it is through this lens that we wrote this book.

> By helping you with new skills, we seek to empower you to create dynamic learning environments that inspire curiosity, promote critical thinking, and prepare students for success in an increasingly complex and interconnected world.

Regardless of your level of experience or your current teaching responsibility, there are times when teachers are tasked with moving onto new and unfamiliar territories. It is for this and many other reasons why being prepared is so important. Adaire's story below highlights the reasons why she felt so passionately about being prepared.

VOICES FROM THE FIELD

The Importance of Being Prepared

Adaire Comeau

As a new teacher, being prepared is the most effective anxiety relief that one can find. This is something that I learned early on, and is undoubtedly the reason that I was able to survive the rollercoaster of the first few years. Within my four years of teaching, I have faced

(Continued)

(Continued)

immense variability. I have navigated through three different high schools, and have taught almost every level of English and social studies (from remedial to academic). Through every school environment and classroom that I have found myself in, I have realized the necessity of showing up prepared to address each new task. Truly, preparedness is a skill that must be developed over time. The rigors of my university education set a strong foundation that was then built on by the exceptional wisdom and materials offered by my colleagues. However, it is important to recognize that preparedness is mostly defined by the work that you put in yourself, and the ability to learn from the mistakes you make as you grow.

Evidently, the pressure to be prepared when teaching classes of 30 (or more) kids may seem like a daunting task. As a fresh university graduate, I remember feeling the sheer weight of the job before me: establishing confidence in the content of my subject area, building engaging materials, knowing how to differentiate those materials depending on the students in my room, being culturally aware and conscious as I plan and bring in new resources, and learning how to deliver all of that in a clear and coherent way. Indeed, it seems rightfully intimidating. What I have found is that the only way to reduce my own stress levels is to ensure that I show up to work every day equipped with the necessary tools to do my job. Unfortunately, this does require personal time and effort, and that is unavoidable. When assuming new teaching roles, it is natural that one will have to undertake additional work to establish their expertise in the field.

Due to this reality, I decided to make it a goal for myself to seek out every learning opportunity possible, so that I could build my own toolkit to prepare for the obstacles that I would surely face. Regularly attending professional development has been instrumental in establishing my confidence in the classroom. Being willing to acknowledge my personal need for growth, and ask for help when I know I am unable to handle a situation on my own has also been especially beneficial. In future years, I plan on continuing to do both of these things as I recognize the fact that frankly, as teachers, learning never stops.

Now, as you embark on your teaching journey, finding your way through this wonderfully challenging job may be difficult. However, having a resource which allows those before you to piece together some of the most important lessons they can offer, is definitely one of the most powerful forms of preparation that I can think of. I truly wish this book existed when I was starting my career, and I hope it serves as a valuable source of knowledge for you moving forward.

THE IMPORTANCE OF USING THIS BOOK IN YOUR PREPARATION

When the four of us sat down to conceptualize how we wanted to share our work with you, the reader, we wanted to share as much as possible. As such you will notice this book has a lot of information from a lot of different places. When reading through each chapter we want to make a few things very clear. Firstly, by no means are you expected to know, understand, and apply everything we wrote in this book in your first year of teaching but rather it is our hope you use this book as a resource or a jumping off point for further professional learning, or professional reading. Secondly, we recognize that each chapter has strategies, information, and stories that are intended to introduce you to new information. If we were to flush out everything we wanted to share with you this book could very well have been 500 pages and we know no new teacher needs a 500-page book on teaching! So if there are things in here that pique your interest, we recommend exploring the topic further and linking with a mentor or colleague to learn more. Use this book as a platform for exploration and learning.

HOW TO USE THIS BOOK

As you embark upon your first days, weeks, and months as a classroom teacher, you will realize that there is always something to learn and work on. In fact, we know that it is truly the first three years of being in the profession that are so critically important to your formation, development, and growth as a teacher. At times, it may seem overwhelming and that there are too many areas to address at once. This is a normal reaction. We all felt this way too! We invite you to trust us when we say you will soon see your growth as you move from one week to the next. As you become more adept at planning, instructing, assessment, classroom management and all the various skills inherent to teaching, you will feel your confidence and capability grow. We want you to flourish and know that you can!

We designed this book to act as a pseudo choose-your-own-adventure type of resource. We know how valuable your time is, and often the hours of the day for any teacher, let alone a newer teacher, seem to wither away with other tasks. We thought the best approach to assist you in your journey would be to create a book with chapters, each of which can stand alone. The chapters can be read in any order (more like a resource than a cover to cover book), within each chapter is a selection of best practices (*toolkit tactics*) that intend to provide strategies, ideas, and perspectives from the authors as well as new teachers who are currently in the classroom.

By all means, you can read this book cover to cover if you like, but we wanted to ensure it was accessible to everyone regardless of how much time they have to dedicate to their reading. The chapters within this book are titled as follows:

1. Equity and Culturally Responsive Practices
2. Well-Being and Balance
3. The First Days: Figuring Out Your New School
4. The Art and Science of Planning and Lesson Design
5. Setting the Stage: The Significance of the Learning Environment for Student Success
6. Instructional Practices: Building a Strong Foundation in the Classroom
7. Assessment: The Measure of Effective Teaching and Learning

Each chapter is important to your development and it is our hope that you will find each chapter valuable to your professional reading. In hopes to help you choose your own adventure, we recommend that you complete the New Teacher Inventory activity. The purpose of this activity is to act as a diagnostic into your previously learned knowledge and to determine your confidence about the practices of a first year teacher. Through this inventory you may decide to read through the chapters in an order that suits you best. **Please note**, we purposely have not included inventory questions for our first chapter, Equity and Culturally Responsive Practices. We feel that this should be the **first** chapter that all new teachers should read, as well as aspects of this chapter will also permeate throughout the rest of the chapters.

NEW TEACHER INVENTORY

To assist you with exploring some key areas of your current skills, we offer this new teacher inventory. This activity will pose a series of questions that focus on aspects of teacher preparation, instructional practice, assessment, the learning environment and other areas essential to your success. You will be invited to read each prompt and score yourself on a 5-point scale that ranges from "I feel totally confident" to "this is totally an area for more growth." We ask you to answer honestly so that you can get a rich sense of what you already do well and help to determine areas of need for growth. You will note that there is a scoring guide, and this will help point you to the relevant chapters of the book where you will find advice, tips, and practical guidance on how to address the areas you have identified for growth. Let's begin!

1. I am completely confident with this.
2. I am familiar with this and am reasonably confident.
3. I am somewhat familiar with this.
4. I am somewhat familiar with this, but I require more learning.
5. This is new to me, and requires significant learning.

Instructions: Read each prompt carefully. Write the number in the blank that corresponds to the 5-point scale above.

1. I am familiar with student conduct, safety, and emergency protocols. ______
2. I can create short-term and long-range learning plans. ______
3. I can utilize a variety of questioning techniques in my instruction. ______
4. I take time to know what my students know prior to teaching them. ______
5. I know how to effectively use formative assessment techniques. ______
6. I ensure I make and take time to look after my own well-being. ______
7. I am familiar with the mission and vision statements of my school. ______

8. I am familiar with district learning resources and supports. ______

9. I am familiar with an array of classroom management strategies. ______

10. I can create a classroom environment that stimulates learning. ______

11. I am conversant with various forms of assessment data. ______

12. I am familiar with the district's health and wellness benefits and services. ______

13. I am familiar with the outcomes and standards of my subject areas. ______

14. I can discern high quality resources from lower quality ones. ______

15. I can scaffold supports for students requiring differentiation. ______

16. I leverage mistakes as opportunities for learning with my students. ______

17. I make good use of feedback in my assessment instruments. ______

18. I intentionally pursue activities outside of work to connect to the community. ______

19. I am familiar with key staff members and who to ask if I need help. ______

20. I know how to access professional development opportunities. ______

21. I can readily provide learning outcomes and success criteria to students. ______

22. I can create a classroom environment that stimulates learning. ______

23. I am comfortable having students cocreate rubrics with me. ______

24. I can establish healthy boundaries in relationships with homelife and work. ______

Add up the scores as follows to determine your score in relation to each of the areas in the following table. Remember the higher the score the more unfamiliar the chapter is to you now, and this would be a priority for learning.

Prompt and Corresponding Chapter	Score
Well-Being and Balance (Chapter 2): 6, 12, 18, 24	
The First Days (Chapter 3): 1, 7, 13, 19	
Planning and Lesson Design (Chapter 4): 2, 8, 14, 20	
Learning Environment (Chapter 5): 4, 10, 16, 22	
Instructional Practice (Chapter 6): 3, 9, 15, 21	
Assessment (Chapter 7): 5, 11,17, 23	

NOW WHAT?

Hopefully the inventory you took gave you some perspective on which chapter you should read first, but in case you may have run into the situation that many of us ran into and you don't know where to begin, we have included a short summary of each chapter in the following table. Feel free to explore this book in any way that you feel would be best to support your thinking, and your growth as a new teacher. After the summaries of each chapter, we have included a space for you to chart some goals, and reflections in preparation for your reading.

Equity and Culturally Responsive Practices	We feel this should be the first chapter you start with regardless of your current level of experience with equity and culturally responsive practices. Equity and culturally responsive practices are intentionally placed at the beginning of this book to highlight the significance of providing a classroom experience where all learners are welcome, and all students feel a sense of identity and belonging in your room.
Well-Being and Balance	Teaching is a rewarding, but tiring career. We included this chapter as a reminder that it's not only ok, but recommended that you take steps to ensure you are taking care of yourself. This is often one of the first things that we forget as we embark in a teaching career. This chapter is intended to remind you of the ways you can maintain your well-being and balance as a new teacher.
The First Days of Teaching	The first days of any new job can be really daunting, let alone a job where you are responsible for teaching a group of kids! This chapter is intended to provide some insights into aspects of the first days that may go unnoticed. There are opportunities in this chapter to connect with colleagues and learn more about your school and community.

Planning and Lesson Design	Planning and lesson design are critical to making learning experiences for students that have impact on their growth and achievement. This chapter explores important aspects of planning, and determining what makes good, better, and best supports for you in the classroom.
The Learning Environment	Where the learning occurs has just as much impact on the students as what and how they are learning. This chapter explores the tangible and intangible aspects of the classroom environment and provides actionable items for you to consider as you design your ideal classroom environment.
Instructional Practices	A well planned lesson can only get you so far in the classroom. This chapter provides considerations for instructional practices that will help boost the impact of your classroom instruction.
Assessment Practices	Oftentimes students can feel that assessments are something that are done to them. This chapter provides insights and practical ways of using assessment practices as means to gather evidence of student learning, rather than cast judgment on their abilities as a learner.

It is truly our hope that this book will support your development as a teacher over the course of your first few years. Part of growth and lifelong learning is being reflective about your learning, and the goals you set for yourself. As such, the box at the end of this section is provided for you to chart your goals for this book. There will be reflective practices embedded throughout each of the chapters to help you think about your own growth along the way. Good luck with your school year, and always remember you are already making more of an impact on students' lives than you will ever know.

WHAT ARE MY THREE MAIN GOALS FOR GROWTH AS I READ THROUGH THIS BOOK?

Goal #1:
Goal #2:
Goal #3:

EQUITY AND CULTURALLY RESPONSIVE PRACTICES

Diversity. Equity. Inclusion. Now, more than ever, this is the work we must embrace in our schools. If we are to help students improve critical thinking, literacy, numeracy, and other essential skills—and become the lifelong learners we aspire to develop—then fostering a sense of belonging and safety is foundational. Every student needs to feel valued and secure, both physically and mentally. Creating classrooms free from racism, bias, and judgment is integral to this mission.

What defines a *teacher*? Some might say a teacher sets rules to ensure safety, while others may see them as facilitators of curriculum or mentors beyond academics. To me, a teacher is someone who inspires and motivates students. Teachers create positive environments where students learn fundamental life and academic skills that prepare them for the future.

As a teacher of color, I felt a deep responsibility to embody these values for all my students. Representation mattered greatly—not just for those who looked like me but for every student in the room. I hope I inspired my students to value diversity and equity and instilled in them the belief that every person deserves to feel seen and respected.

Our actions as teachers can make a profound difference, positively or negatively. The work of creating inclusive, equitable classrooms is not easy, and it can feel daunting. Many teachers fear making mistakes that could offend or upset others. However, the stakes are too high to let fear hold us back. If we, as educators with institutional support, feel overwhelmed, imagine the burden placed on young people who are uncertain about their value and security. They need us to lead.

Representation in the classroom extends beyond race. For instance, a book about the famous Canadian soccer player Alphonso Davies isn't just for Black students—it's for anyone who identifies with his journey, whether as a soccer player, a refugee, or a young person striving against the odds. This kind of representation allows students to see themselves and others in meaningful, multifaceted ways. It's a reminder that diversity includes ethnicity, ability, gender, religion, language, and interests.

Equity means fairness, while equality means treating everyone the same. To illustrate, imagine a footrace: Equality is giving everyone the same size-12 shoes, regardless of whether they fit. Equity is ensuring each runner has shoes that fit perfectly. In the classroom, equity might mean providing speech-to-text tools, a translator, a quiet workspace, or a scribe to meet the unique needs of each student. Equity ensures all students have the opportunity to succeed and feel confident in their abilities. By meeting students where they are, we create a classroom community where every child feels valued and capable of achieving their best.

Culturally responsive teaching helps students explore their own heritage while learning about the backgrounds of others. This approach goes beyond race—it considers abilities, languages, body sizes, and other dimensions of diversity to ensure every child feels seen and valued. It's not about division but connection, helping students build empathy and a sense of community.

True, avoiding this work might feel safer, but just as ships are safest in harbor, that's not where they're meant to stay—and neither are you. You became a teacher to make a difference in students' lives. This is your chance. It's the gift and responsibility of teaching: to be a difference maker in the life of a child.

We recognize that DEI work can feel overwhelming, and mistakes are inevitable. However, mistakes made with a good heart and thoughtful preparation are forgivable. Lean on your mentors, school leaders, colleagues, and resources like this book. Most importantly, listen to your students—they will provide honest feedback and guidance if you pay attention. They want you to succeed because they want to have a teacher who notices and values them for who they are.

Equity in education is not about perfection but progress. It's about creating spaces where every child feels safe, valued, and empowered to thrive. By embracing diversity, practicing cultural responsiveness, and prioritizing equity, you can move the needle in meaningful ways.

Remember, you are not alone in this work. Seek out conversations, reflect on feedback, and continue learning. Ask questions, read widely, and stay curious. The effort you put into fostering equity and inclusion in your classroom will have a lasting impact—not just on your students but on the future they will help shape.

As you embark through the rest of this chapter, we wanted to make sure you had a clear map of the concepts and ideas that will be explored more in depth. As we mentioned previously in the introduction, do not feel pressured to try and apply all of these ideas, rather explore as many of these as you can and apply what piques your interests or needs. Enjoy exploring the following toolbox tactics:

1. Ensuring Everyone Is Heard and Listened To: Building a classroom where everyone feels they belong is critical to student success.
2. Are You "New" Here or Do You "Know" Here?: Understanding and acknowledging your relationship with your context is a key part of your success.
3. Just Say Hello: Getting to know your students is vital to their success and yours.
4. Equitable Access and Opportunity: Creating a learning community where everyone feels they can succeed is paramount to achievement.
5. DEI Burnout: Managing yours and others expectations is vital to your long-term success as a teacher.
6. Getting to Know Your Students: Teaching is about building rapport and mutual understanding, a sure way to be successful in the classroom.

TOOLKIT TACTIC 1.1 ENSURING EVERYONE IS HEARD AND LISTENED TO

***Case**: There is a difference between listening to someone and truly listening to someone. Hearing someone ensures that you know what they want or need, but there is a feeling of action that is tied to listening. For example, you may hear a student say, "I like soccer," and you respond accordingly. As teachers, we take action when we hear sentences like this. Listening to a student who tells you they like soccer may result in you finding an extra soccer ball for the recess bin, including books about soccer in your classroom library, or structuring a physical education class accordingly. Both skills are of importance and it is important to continue to use our judgment to hear and to listen.*

***From Wayne**: Self-admittedly, my first few weeks and months of teaching were not great. I was nervous and wanted to do well. I planned and executed my lessons but nothing seemed to hit all that well with the students. It was not until I finally began to really listen to what my students were telling me through their actions and words that I began to figure out how to truly meet their needs. They wanted more about their own history and community in my social studies lesson. Once I made that connection, things went much better. Listen first, then act.*

AUTHOR'S CORNER

Sarah's Experience

I was lucky to teach in an elementary school for eight years. In those eight years, I taught Grades 3 through 6, and had the ability to teach many students twice, and even, three times. One of those students is named Kenisha.

In my third year of teaching Grade 3, a beautiful, Haitian-Canadian girl walked into my classroom and her eyes lit up at seeing me, a young Ghanaian-Canadian woman, as her homeroom teacher. We connected immediately over things like music, hair products, and cultural snacks. One of the first activities planned for our class was to create a life-size self-portrait to surround the perimeter of our classroom. After working very hard, Kenisha approached me and said, "I'm done, Miss Adomako!" What she handed me was not even close to what she looked like; her depiction of herself was blonde, blue eyed, and had white skin. When I asked her why, she replied, "I want to be pretty, like *them*," and pointed to a group of young girls who represented what she created. After a quick pep talk about how beautiful she is in the skin that she is in, and a promise to put her self-portrait next to mine, she redid her portrait to represent her. Those portraits stayed up for the entire year, and were taken down in June and given to students to do what they wished with them.

Three years later, I taught Kenisha again, in Grade 6. It was a pleasure to see her again, a little taller, a little sassier, but the same level of excitement to see a teacher that looked like her. On our first day back, she gave me a hug and reminded me of the self-portrait project, but confided in me that she kept hers in her bedroom with affirmations to constantly remind herself that she is beautiful, smart, and worthy. Moments like this helped remind me of the importance of my presence in the classroom, and continue to remind me why my existence is important in the field of education.

BUILDING CLASSROOM COMMUNITY

One of the skills that is paramount as a teacher is, not only listening to, but considering all voices. The students in your class have thoughts and opinions and, especially in the beginning days of school, considering their thoughts and ideas will help shape and build an inclusive classroom for all. On the first day in your classroom, it's important to build a classroom community that promotes friendship, inclusivity, and kindness. Additionally, your classroom community should create an atmosphere where students feel both brave and safe. One of my goals as a teacher was to create a space for my students that was comfortable and fun, but also a place that was okay to be incorrect, a place that was okay to have differing opinions and thoughts, and a place in which questioning and inquiry were things that were celebrated. My classroom had a combination of single desks as well as tables. The single desks could be moved into groups and could be solo work stations. Students were encouraged to work together in some situations, but also encouraged to learn to work on their own. Our classroom "rules" were called a *promise* and conversations were had regarding things we could all agree to, things like, keeping the room clean, lifting others up, listening when someone is speaking, and not interfering with the learning of others. Hearing from students on what is important to them regarding their learning space and their relationships with one another helped keep them accountable if and when things, inevitably, went sideways. Redirection was necessary and often; at least once a month, we would review our classroom promise and discuss its importance. Coconstructing this document was key because we took into consideration everything that we agreed as a class was of importance to us and, again, helped to keep everyone accountable.

When shaping your classroom community, ask students what they want to see. Perhaps they want books with protagonists that look like them. Maybe they would like visual aids in math. Have you considered a cozy corner for reading and working? Students will take pride in their work, their space, and in one other, when given the opportunity to share and collaborate. Ultimately, the decisions made for the greater good of the classroom are yours, but it doesn't hurt to consult the students to see how they may be best supported. All of these things will help to shape your classroom community and make it a place that students want to come back day after day.

QUESTIONS TO ASK YOUR MENTOR OR COLLEAGUES

Ultimately, you are the classroom teacher. You have many responsibilities in the run of a day, and it's incredibly important that students feel safe, supported, and cared for in your presence. Do you have questions for your mentor? Here are some things that may be specific to your school board:

- What is the best way to showcase representation in our school community?
- Are there things I should take into consideration when celebrating culture?
- What does our school already do to showcase culture within the curriculum?
- What tools exist for students who require differentiation in their learning?

SELF-REFLECTION (POST-READING)

How might you connect with students in a culturally responsive way?

In what ways can you bring more equitable learning opportunities to your classroom?

TOOLKIT TACTIC 1.2 ARE YOU "NEW" HERE OR DO YOU "KNOW" HERE?

Case: *A new adventure begins at the start of each school year. Whether this is your first year of teaching or your first year in a different school, there is so much to know. Many considerations like location, demographic, family structures, community members, and more, are important to take into account. It is important to connect with other teachers and school staff in the building to find out the ins and outs of your new school.*

From Vince: *My first teaching assignment was at an academically focused high school, where students maintained very high expectations of themselves and their teachers. Not knowing this at first, I remember teaching a 12th grade IB class. Over the course of the first week, I realized very quickly that my students were hungry for as much information as possible, and it felt like they were all smarter than me! This forced me to quickly adjust my instruction and ensure I had a firm grasp of my content. My students pushed me just as much as I pushed them!*

WHAT DO YOU ALREADY KNOW?

SCHOOL STORIES

Mrs. Enright

"Teaching at the same school as my sister has been such a blessing! I had the opportunity to have her as my mentor coming into a new school and I am so grateful that I had her around to help me ease into this new building. I am coming from a very affluent, well-off community to a more inner-city school. She told me immediately that teaching will be different here. I used to assign a lot of things online. She told me that a lot of students at this school don't have internet access at home or share one Chromebook with three or four other siblings, all with homework. Most families at this school get holiday hampers because money is really tight. Sometimes students come to school and their main priority is to eat. All of these things are so different from what I am used to but I see how much my sister loves this school and all of the students she teaches. They really love her and I hope I fit in here too."

Despite coming from a community that is different from what she knows, Mrs. Enright took the time to find out from another teacher, in this case, her sister, what her new (to her) school will be like. Getting to know the community you will work in, the demographic, and some of the soft needs of the community, like food scarcity, potential poverty, hygiene, lack of access to resources, and more, is very important. Coming into a situation such as this is great to know ahead of time in order to prepare. You may decide to print more so as to eliminate the use of devices constantly in the classroom. You may start a breakfast or snack program or find donations in order to provide food for students. As we know, students who are hungry can't learn. Knowing information like this ahead of time is great to know so that you can ask administrators or other teachers for the best ways to support the students in your class. On the flip side, you may be entering a school that is the opposite of a situation like this. Perhaps all of your students have every device known to man and can afford to bring the most elaborate lunches and snacks to school. These things don't necessarily mean that you need to change your teaching practice drastically. At the end of the day, when students come to school, they are all responsible for learning curricular outcomes, learning soft skills like kindness and empathy, and learning to work collaboratively with others. This may not have anything to do with demographics, but as the teacher, it is your job to ensure that every child feels like they can do anything when they are in your room; some just may need a snack first.

WHAT DO YOU NEED TO LEARN?

Oftentimes, in the first few days of school without students, there are meetings and onboarding professional development opportunities. These benefit new and returning teachers and school staff alike. If you are a teacher that is new, you will learn an overwhelming amount of information regarding the area that you now teach in. If you are not paired with a mentor teacher at this time, don't be shy to ask for one. Teachers that have been at the school longer than you have will know better about how to support some of the more intricate needs of the students that are there. Specific school staff, like the administrative support or educational assistants, will know particular information regarding certain students or families in your classroom. It's important for you to know these things, if they pertain to you as their homeroom, language, or option teacher, so that you can find ways to support students who may require more accommodations.

You may teach at a school with cultural or religious significance. If you are not from that community, it doesn't hurt to learn a bit about the culture or religion of the students of the community. It's easy to learn the "rules" regarding going to a mosque, for example, but learning some of the intimate details, like the significance of certain prayers, or foods eaten during certain times of year, will prove to be incredibly meaningful to the students you serve. Better yet, asking the students if they would like to share that information with you is very special. Students love any opportunity to relate to their teacher and reverse roles. Allowing students to be the teacher in things that make up their identity is just another way to demonstrate culturally responsive pedagogy. You cannot possibly be the expert in every realm; allow students to share the things they may be the expert in.

SEEK OUT COMMUNITY

Schools are becoming more diverse, year after year. There are students making their homes in North America who may be coming from countries around the world. All of these students come to us with language, celebrations, food, cultural dress, songs, and faith; they may also come with generational trauma, war, crime, and poverty. As mentioned earlier, you cannot possibly be the expert in all of these things.

Parents, grandparents, cultural elders, and community helpers are always looking for a way to connect with student learning opportunities. Currently, in Canada, the nation is undergoing a time of reconciliation regarding Indigenous heritage and identity. As a nation, citizens are learning and becoming more aware of the injustices that have happened toward Indigenous peoples for hundreds of years. I am someone who's ancestry is from Ghana in West Africa; I do not have Indigenous roots. It's of the utmost importance, however, to teach students about the things in the country's history that aren't written in the textbook to bring the truth to light. I could do a lot of research on my own, but I find that I often lean on Indigenous learning groups and invite Indigenous Elders and community speakers into the classroom. The lessons taught are authentic and meaningful coming from someone of the community. Students can ask questions that perhaps I cannot answer; that's definitely okay.

Inviting community into the classroom is a wonderful way to connect students with other cultural leaders and teachers who may look like them. The lessons that they may bring into the classroom can always be tied to curricular outcomes, however, sometimes it's important for students to just listen and learn, not for a report card mark.

HOW WILL YOU INTERACT WITH THE COMMUNITY?

As an educator, you have the unique opportunity to make a meaningful impact not only within the walls of your classroom but also in the broader community. Take advantage of this opportunity by actively engaging with students, families, and community partners. Think about attending local events such as community sporting events, festivals, or cultural gatherings. This quickly demonstrates your interest in the community goes beyond "the job" at the school and shows your personal investment in becoming part of the community. It will also provide opportunities to meet students and their families in a relaxed atmosphere where you can all get to know each other a bit better. However, just do not forget you are always a teacher and discussing students or colleagues or indulging in questionable behaviors is never defensible, even if you view it as being off the clock.

You can also consider volunteering your time and expertise to support local initiatives such as food drives, tutoring programs, or community clean-up efforts. By demonstrating your commitment to serving others, you not only enrich the educational experience for your students but also inspire them to become active and engaged citizens.

QUESTIONS TO ASK YOUR MENTOR OR COLLEAGUES

Consider asking the following things to a mentor or your administrator. It's never too late to learn something new about your new school community; however, take the time to know the community around you and talk to other school staff to see what they may do in situations that arise:

- What cultures are represented in the school?
- Are there any situations regarding any of the students or the families in my classroom?
- What can you tell me about the demographics of this area?
- What supports (mental health, hygiene, nutritional, cultural, etc.) exist for the students in this school?
- What gifts and skills do you bring to the school?
- How can I be of better service to the families in this school community?

SELF-REFLECTION (POST-READING)

Who can you turn to for support in your new school community?

What is the demographic of the school you are teaching in? Do the students and families you serve require extra support?

What is something you need to learn about to better serve the students in your new school community?

TOOLKIT TACTIC 1.3 JUST SAY HELLO

Case: *You are a difference maker. Read that again. Yes, you. Just like those awesome teachers that inspired you to take up the challenge. Your approach to the day and how you greet the students will communicate to them a great many things. The first impression will happen every day—use it wisely!*

From Sarah: *There is power within connection. Saying hello is a simple yet powerful gesture that helps teachers build positive relationships with their students. My third-grade teacher, Mrs. Gwen Davies, made it her mission to give us all a resounding hello and good morning each day. It was often paired with a chapter out of a Roald Dahl novel; my favourite was* The BFG. *By doing this, she set a welcoming tone, fostered a sense of belonging for us, and created an environment that showed us that she cared about us. A friendly greeting can brighten a student's day and even enhance their motivation to learn; I know it did for me. Thank you, Mrs. Davies, for a year of hellos, good mornings, and character voices as we settled in for a busy day of learning.*

Every day, students will arrive at school in a variety of states. Some will have had breakfast, been told multiple times they are loved, and told to have a good day by the person or people who take care of them. Some will not. Some will have had tougher mornings. Some will have had no one there to greet them when they got themselves out of bed and perhaps also had to get their siblings up and out the door too. Some will have been told they are no good or be under immense pressure to perform at a level that makes their stomach churn, invoking a state of anxiety that many of us are unable to fathom. Some will be worried that you will notice they are still wearing the same shirt from yesterday. Some will dread every step of the walk to school, concerned that the lunch their caregiver or parents made for them will smell a bit too much or be made fun of by their classmates. Some will worry that their accent sounds funny or that their name is just too hard for you to pronounce and instead you will go with the "English version." Some will dread special days that highlight only too clearly that their family does not fit the "norm" although we are not sure anyone knows what that looks like today. Others will be thinking about the excuse they will give when the next field trip rolls around and they know they cannot come up with the cash so a sick day will have to suffice.

Now maybe you can see these groups of students in your mind's eye. The visualizations you construct will be based on many things: your own and other's experiences, your knowledge of the world through media, your biases and assumptions.

Thus, the first part of this strategy is to put those preconceived ideas aside. Most of them will be wrong and if for some reason they are correct, they will be of little use to you. They will limit your ability to be what the students need—for you to be present and as unconditionally welcoming as possible as they enter the learning space for another day of engagement. These assumptions will also limit your ability to see the students for who they are—a group of children simply bringing their best selves every day. Yes, you will have photocopying to do. You will also have last-second prepping and marking to sneak in. These are things that will always be there for you. However, each morning you will have just one chance to greet your students—to be a difference maker—to set the tone for the day ahead. To say hello and communicate to them they each matter, that they are safe and they belong. It will be up to you how boisterous or animated you want to be and how much the students can handle. You will also have learned what practices are acceptable and appropriate based on your students' backgrounds. But if you can do your best to be there to say hello, greet them by name, and welcome them to the learning space you will have gone a long way to helping them succeed, where kids can come, engage, be themselves, and safely and confidently share who they are.

SELF-REFLECTION (POST-READING)

When you come upon a student in the hallway, do you just walk past, or do you acknowledge them or do you wait for them to make the first move? Does it matter? If they are not in your class, so what? What if you say hello and they do not respond?

TOOLBOX TACTIC 1.4 EQUITABLE ACCESS AND OPPORTUNITY

Case: *It is important that all students have the resources and opportunities they need to succeed. And while schools will offer some levels of programming and resources for students it is incumbent on you as the classroom teacher to learn your students and their needs. However, caregivers and parents are relying on you to make good decisions with their children and to read the situation and stay within the community parameters when it comes to cost and risk. Thus, the actions you take must ensure a level of equity is maintained in your learning space and that all students feel part of the team.*

From Tim: *I remember taking my students to the local arena for skating lessons. One student who was wheelchair bound would stay back at the school and do some alternate assignment while we were away. This stuck with me. How would I feel if I was relegated to the sidelines like that? With discussion and persistence, my principal and the student's parents supported me in bringing the student to the rink and getting them on the ice. I learned that with equity you don't need to see it to believe it, rather when you believe in it, you will see it.*

Equity in access to resources and opportunities is foundational to DEI. This involves recognizing and addressing systemic barriers that may affect certain groups of students such as inclusive practices in the classroom, resource allocation and keeping a very careful eye on discipline practices to ensure they are equitable.

Implementing classroom strategies that accommodate diverse needs, such as flexible seating arrangements, varied instructional materials, and accessible technology is important to the success of your students. But how do you do that? A great first step, if you are unsure, is talking to your mentor or a divisional consultant if one is available. A valuable tool in this pursuit is stepping outside of yourself and trying to gain the perspective of each student. Walking to the back of the classroom and sitting at the desk farthest away from you, can you read what you wrote on the board? Have you talked to student services in your school so you know who might need extra support or even a closer seat?

As you begin the year, think about the equitable distribution of resources, such as technology, books, and other learning aids in your classroom. Asking yourself if you have ensured all students have what they need to succeed is critical. Being aware that this will most likely change each day and as the year goes on, depending on what and who you are teaching is also important. And knowing that your time with each student is a valuable resource is also a sign that you are understanding your importance in the learning environment.

A further important point for you as an emerging teacher to consider is how and to who you apply discipline. No doubt as a new teacher, you will experience frustration as you learn the art of classroom management. The students will most likely test you as well, trying to figure you out, especially considering the fact you are new to them. Thus, being very aware of who and how you are applying discipline to is important. Again, we circle back to earlier points made in this chapter about understanding your biases and to a large extent you own triggers.

FIELD TRIPPING: 360 DEGREES OF PLANNING

Field trips represent valuable learning opportunities that not only enhance but directly facilitate student learning. However, venturing outside the school requires careful and comprehensive planning. As a teacher and field trip organizer, you must consider all aspects and start preparations early. A 360-degree approach addresses educational objectives and the socioeconomic, cognitive, and other needs of students and their families. This holistic strategy ensures that all students can fully participate and benefit from the experience.

CONNECTING TO LEARNING OBJECTIVES

Firstly, aligning the educational goals of the field trip with classroom outcomes and standards is crucial for gaining support from school leadership and parents, especially if you request funds. Whether it's a day trip to see a local food bank in operation, engaging with scientific exhibits, or an overnight trip to a regional music fest, the trip must enhance classroom learning and provide hands-on, experiential opportunities. Another consideration is the impact of your trip on your colleagues and how taking the students might impact on their lesson planning. Good communication is key to strong relationships with your colleagues.

SOCIOECONOMIC CONSIDERATIONS

When considering potential destinations, be mindful of the socio-economic backgrounds of your students. Field trips can be costly, and asking students to request money from their parents should be approached sensitively. Making assumptions about families' financial capabilities can be disastrous to your credibility as a teacher. Explore cost-effective alternatives, such as applying for grants, partnering with community organizations, fundraising, or seeking support from the parent association. Consider transportation logistics and look for the most cost-effective way to get the job done. Inform parents early so they have time to budget, and be prepared to discuss financial assistance for those who need it.

LOOKING AFTER COGNITIVE AND PHYSICAL NEEDS

Collaborate with student services to assess the cognitive and physical needs of your students. Ensure the destination is accessible and that students of all abilities can participate. Plan for differentiated instruction and provide materials at varying levels. For students with specific cognitive needs, prepare guides or pre-trip materials to help them understand and anticipate the experience. Remember, leaving a student behind is not an option; you are the teacher to all students and must include everyone in the trip. Imagine watching all your colleagues leave for a professional development opportunity and you were told you had to stay behind. Not a great feeling and one that you do not want to be remembered for causing.

NUTS AND BOLTS

Finally, plan every detail. Create an itemized agenda with phone numbers, maps, contact information for students, and other essentials. Ensure tickets are purchased, tour entry times are confirmed, and conduct a walk-through of the locations if possible. The complexity and duration of the trip will dictate the extent of your planning. A local park study for a Grade 4 biology class will require different planning than a five-day high school civics bus trip to the national capital. Always prioritize safety by consulting and adhering to school, district, and other relevant policies and procedures.

ENGAGING FAMILIES

Involve families in the planning process, helping them secure funds and building enthusiasm to encourage reluctant students. Inform them well in advance about the trip, its objectives, and the benefits for their children. Invite family members to participate as chaperones, clarifying the requirements and selection process if more volunteers apply than needed. This could include helping with preparations or bringing specific knowledge to enhance the experience.

PREPARING THE STUDENTS

Some students may become anxious as the trip approaches. Prepare them emotionally and socially by discussing behavior expectations. Provide pre-trip information and activities that build excitement and context, such as photos, websites, and videos. These resources can reduce the unknown for students and build anticipation. For overnight trips, additional preparation may be necessary to help students feel comfortable being away from home.

By adopting a 360-degree planning approach, you can ensure that field trips are enriching, inclusive, and accessible for all students. This comprehensive strategy not only meets educational goals but also addresses the diverse needs of students and their families, creating a positive and memorable learning experience.

TOOLBOX TACTIC 1.5 DEI BURNOUT

Case: *This toolbox tactic will resonate most with people who cross multiple intersections; ethnicity, gender, ability, or disability. However, this toolbox tactic is important for all teachers to consider.*

From Sarah: *Burnout related to DEI work happens often with folks from equity-deserving communities. The ability to help and support the learning for people who aren't marginalized is necessary, but the teaching shouldn't fall solely on their shoulders. Something for all of us to consider is that months of recognition, for example, Black History Month in February, should be a month of celebration, not a burden for folks who celebrate. DEI burnout often affects those most committed to creating inclusive environments, especially individuals from marginalized groups who may already face systemic challenges. Share the responsibility; continue to learn.*

There is a joke that circulated online in 2020 that went something like, "If you are a person of color, queer, or have a disability of any kind, you might as well put 'DEI Consultant' on your resume, because you'll be treated like one." Unknowingly, this became reality for many teachers that fit in one or more of these categories, myself included. Suddenly,

I was hearing from teachers across the province about how they are being asked major queries and questions regarding racism, homophobia, and ableism. They were being asked to champion causes for simply being a part of a community. They were being assigned things like cultural events, clubs, and pride celebrations because these things may be a part of their identity. As I'm sure you can see, this is problematic. The question that may follow is "Why?"

Oftentimes, people who are white are looking for permission or support in displaying allyship to people from equity-deserving groups. There are several things that can be done to ensure that people from equity-deserving groups stay in the roles that they are in, are comfortable in those roles, and aren't given roles or tasks that feed stereotypes:

- *Do the learning unprompted*: Folks who are in an equity-deserving intersection are looking to be seen as learners, not the expert and spokesperson for their group. There are many books, articles, and podcasts that can be consumed on why Reconciliation is important to Canadians, or why you shouldn't touch a Black person's hair, spontaneously and without asking. There are many resources that exist to support the learning of folks looking to do better for those around them. Through simple Google searches or many equity-based social media accounts as a guide, you can tap into a world of resources and commentary on how to continuously include, uplift, and support people who may look and act differently than you. This includes our students—some students will enter the classroom trying out different names or identities. The ability to uplift and support students in their own learning about themselves and their culture is a part of our responsibility that shouldn't be taken lightly.
- *Take on some of the load*: Instead of asking the people of color in your staff meeting to lead a schoolwide multicultural day event or a daily lunch club exclusive to girls, for example, ask how you can take some of that load from them. By simply asking, "What can I do to support you?" or, "How can I make this task less work for you?" Simple things like offering to host a club in your classroom, co-leading an activity, or jumping on a committee for a group that you may not be a part of is an incredible way to demonstrate allyship and not add to the burnout that your colleagues may be facing.
- *Collaborate with others*: After doing some learning about different groups, take the lead! It may seem as though you are taking over, but, on the contrary. Allyship to equity-deserving groups is a great way to aid in lightening the load for others. Students of color need to

see teachers who look like them in spaces like this; additionally, students of color need to see teachers who do not look like them championing them, their culture, and their interests. One of the things I strived to do was learn to say, "Hello," in the languages of each of my students. Even though I am not Cree, Ukrainian, or Filipino, learning how to say that simple greeting was a great way to encourage and model collaboration and acceptance to my students. Additionally, reaching out to community members on how they can collaborate to bring culture to students is a truly authentic and meaningful way to help support the growth, learning, and positive response toward diversity in schools.

If you're looking for a sign to start, here it is. Learning different ways to support your colleagues in equity-deserving groups is the most wonderful way to show allyship. People of color, queer people, and people with different abilities aren't looking for you to yell from the rooftops; on the contrary, they are simply looking for more people to join them in creating more inclusive and accepting spaces to learn about one another.

TOOLBOX TACTIC 1.6 GETTING TO KNOW YOUR STUDENTS

Case: *We know that our students and colleagues come from increasingly diverse backgrounds. Being able to understand, respect, and effectively interact with your students is important. Recognizing and appreciating students' cultural differences and building this knowledge into your classroom and teaching practices will be helpful. Asking questions and doing research will be necessary for you to build your abilities to support all students in a respectful manner.*

From Vince: *There is school culture, and there is my role in the school culture. In many ways, there always will be an intersection between the culture of the school and the cultures that exist within the culture of the school. It was so important for me to learn about all the unique and wonderfully diverse cultures of my students to make sure I was cognizant of the intersectionality that existed between my students as people and the building that serves them.*

You may not be in a new community but nevertheless the students that enter your classroom are each new to you, just as you and your many colleagues are. They may live in the same neighborhood, play for the same community teams, and have many of the same experiences with their families but there will always be a level of uniqueness to each and every student's story. They will need to feel seen, understood, appreciated and welcomed, inclusive of their diverse backgrounds. Your ability to do this will help determine your effectiveness as their teacher.

Cultural competence involves recognizing, respecting, and valuing differences in culture, language, and the rich experiences students and their families come from. It is vital that you recognize and deal with any biases or preconceived ideas that may have previously influenced your thinking especially when it comes to how students learn and behave. As you will learn, navigating and celebrating these differences is crucial to your success.

1. **Self-awareness**: Do you know who you are as a teacher? Start by reflecting on your own cultural identities and biases. Understanding how your own personal experiences and education shape your perceptions and interactions with students is important. This can be disconcerting as you confront your beliefs, but as you will see, it will be a valuable activity.

2. **Active Learning**: What do you know about the community you are working in? How about the students? Do not rely simply on personal observations. Find a person you can trust and ask questions. Start with simpler, straightforward questions and as you build community, move to more complex questions that help give you insight on how to best support your students. Many of your students would love to give you a tour of the neighborhood, a history lesson in the community, or tell you many other details. Other activities could involve reading, attending workshops, or engaging with community resources and leaders.

3. **Building Relationships**: Are you open to getting to know your students and their community? Getting to know the parents and caregivers of your students begins with you. Make the first move! At "Meet the Staff Night," will you stand against the wall with other staff or walk over to parents and engage them in conversation? Making meaningful connections with students and their families will help you later on. And if you have done your homework and understand and recognize some community cultural norms, your actions will be further appreciated.

It is important to remember that developing cultural competence, just like any competence, is an incremental process that you must take ownership over. Think of it as a continuum and that while not everyone is at or even beginning at the same place, we can all do things that make us more capable, more understanding, more fluent in working with all of our students. Thus, even if you feel like you are at the beginning of this process, you can create a classroom environment where all students feel seen and valued, setting the stage for successful learning.

AUTHOR'S CORNER

A Moment in Practice for Wayne

When I (Wayne) began my career, I was in an isolated Indigenous community on the northwest shore of British Columbia, Canada, almost two thousand miles from home. I was new to the community and to teaching. I was also new to living in an Indigenous community. I recognized I had much to learn not just about my teaching but also about the Tsimshian people that lived there. Luckily, I made friends with a local family who took me under their wing. They introduced me to community members and had me to their home many times. They got me a spot on a team in the local basketball league, took me salmon and halibut fishing, and I even went to a community feast as their guest.

When we first met, it was all about the niceties. I met their children and extended family. As time went on, we exchanged observations about the world and many of my preconceived notions were dispelled while others of a more factual variety grew in their place. When I was confused, I asked questions and they helped me by being preemptive in some of the advice they gave. They exploded stereotypes and gave me credibility in the community that allowed me to flourish as a teacher. Now, over three decades later we still are close; we still communicate over the thousands of miles that now separates us since I eventually returned home.

TRY IT: A CONVERSATION

As you begin to find your feet on your new staff, try and get to know another teacher or staff member who grew up in the area. Try to foster a relationship that allows you to work with them to understand the community and most importantly, the students and their families. Be open and honest that you are trying to understand the community so you can better support students. Ask questions but remember this is not an interrogation, it is a conversation over time. Start small and work up to the complex. Here are some examples of deeper questions that you can work up to:

- What are a few things a new teacher could benefit from knowing about the history of this community and how it impacts this school and the students and families it serves, that might not be readily apparent?
- What do you think are the key cultural characteristics of our student population and the greater community?
- What are some community dynamics, events, or traditions that are particularly important to our students and their families?
- What is the history of the relationship between the school (or education in general) and parents and families?
- What advice can you give me on entering this community especially in the capacity of a new teacher?

BRINGING IT ALL TOGETHER

Bringing diversity and equity into your classroom can only shed a positive light on the students that you serve. Thus, as this chapter draws to a close, it is important to reflect on the strategies and approaches discussed. Building a classroom community starts with ensuring every voice is heard and valued, fostering an environment where everyone feels a sense of belonging. By asking questions of your fellow community members and self-reflecting, you will gain insights needed to navigate your classroom and all those who are working and learning within it.

For you to understand the nuances of being "new" versus "knowing" your space is critical to establishing meaningful connections with your students, their families and your peers. By leveraging what you already know and looking for opportunities to learn, you can demonstrate to the community around you that you are interested in meeting them where they are. This means you must get past "your plan" and ask others what they need and then incorporate those thoughts and feelings into "our plan."

Planning with specific purpose, whether for a lesson or a field trip across town, needs careful attention to a variety of factors such as socioeconomic, physical, cultural, or cognitive, in addition to ensuring alignment with the content standards. To make this process easier, engaging with families, preparing students, and knowing who you are and your limits is vital to everyone's success. While all of this may be new to you; that is okay. A successful teacher's learning is ongoing. As we learn better ways to support our students, it is our job as teachers and school staff to help them with those challenges. This cooperative work will only strengthen the bonds we create with our students. At the end of the day, beginning by building a solid foundation of relationships grounded in respect for all members of the learning community in terms of who they are and the perspectives they bring will make you a better teacher.

At the end of each chapter, we have included what we are calling an "implementation tracker." This tool is for you to simply keep track of the tactics that we have shared, and enable you to be mindful of how you might implement them in your practice. It's also worth noting that perhaps not all of these will pertain to your classroom context, so use the tracker to reflect upon which tactics were more impactful for you.

IMPLEMENTATION TRACKER

<table>
<tr><td colspan="2">Attempted toolbox tactic:</td></tr>
<tr><td>Successes:</td><td>Roadblocks:</td></tr>
<tr><td colspan="2">What should I change to be more successful next time?</td></tr>
</table>

Attempted toolbox tactic:	
Successes:	Roadblocks:
What should I change to be more successful next time?	

2

WELL-BEING AND BALANCE

What comes to mind when you think of balance? I (Sarah) will be honest with you, I used to roll my eyes. I used to tell myself that balance was a myth; that it didn't exist. I often wondered how my friends and colleagues would teach all day, and still find the energy to pick up their children from school, take their children to a lesson or a practice, mark an assignment or two, make dinner, eat dinner, do some form of exercise or movement, and spend time with their partner. When I first started teaching, I was single, childless, and living with my parents, and was at school until at least 6:00 p.m., only to continue working at home after eating dinner. To make matters worse, I would go in on Sunday to prepare for the week ahead. Looking back, I couldn't tell you what on Earth I was doing in those moments in my classroom on Sundays, but I knew that I felt like I had to be there. It just didn't seem realistic. With time, my health and physical activity decreased. I was ordering food instead of grocery shopping and cooking healthy meals. I was running on a combination of tea, coffee, and apple juice; not a drop of water consumed until noon.

What I realize now, is that those were the things I thought I needed to be a more productive (read: better) teacher for the students in front of me. My actions resulted, in the short term, in me being tired, feeling sluggish and grumpy, and burnout. Ultimately, I was not the best teacher I could be for my students because I wasn't taking care of myself. Consider where you are in your career. Whether you are in your first year of teaching, first year at a new-to-you school, or have been teaching for many years, take the time to consider what balance looks like for you. This is not to say never drink coffee again or you're a bad teacher if you don't have a salad for lunch daily; on the contrary. This is to remind you to take care of yourself so that you can take care of the students in front of you, enhance their learning, and continue to create and foster positive relationships every day, while taking a break when you need to. This includes setting appropriate boundaries for yourself to ensure you are sustaining yourself through the school year. There is no doubt that the feeling of "more should be done" will live in the back of your mind throughout the year, but it is important to recognize that you need to set up and maintain healthy boundaries between yourself and your work. After all, we are no good to our students if we have not been good to ourselves. In their study of 19 countries and regions Nalipay, King, and Cai (2024) asserted that promoting teacher well-being can positively influence student well-being and overall school climate.

Part of your well-being and balance is understanding that there will be times when you may question your skills and abilities as a new teacher. We want you to know that this is a completely normal feeling, and one that is a natural part of your development as a teacher. Afterall, we are sure you wouldn't be worried, if you didn't want to be the best version of a teacher for your students.

VOICES FROM THE FIELD

Navigating Imposter Phenomenon

E. Schaerer

As someone who is a chronic overthinker, I constantly think of every way I can fail: *What if I'm not prepared? What if my student's scores are below average? What if students hate me? What if everyone sees me as the imposter I perceive myself to be?* I doubt my intellect, my ability, and my competence. At times, I am overcome with self-doubt that results in anxiety.

When I started both my teaching practicums, I felt unprepared. I knew how to construct a ten-page lesson plan, but there was no practical application. *What did being a real teacher constitute? Will the students see right through me? Will the students know that I don't know everything?* In my first year of teaching, like many others who struggle with Imposter Phenomenon, I struggled with perfectionism, and a fear of failure. I denied my own competence, and overcompensated with excessive planning that resulted in burnout. I did not trust myself and my abilities. I would like to say that one day I woke up, began to trust myself and my intuition. However, there was no day or moment that changed this perception. It has taken years of work, guidance under exceptional mentors, and professional development to feel resolve.

The biggest piece of advice I can give to those struggling, is to lean into the Imposter Phenomenon. When you acknowledge that you are not always right—that there are things you do not know—you are humanized in the eyes of your students; it makes you a better teacher. When you acknowledge that you do not know everything, you open yourself up to lifelong learning. My desire to pursue education and lifelong learning is what drives me to be a good teacher. I accept what I do not know and make space for what I will learn.

As an English teacher, there have been moments where students explored aspects of a literary text that I had not thoroughly examined. Initially, I felt incompetent; I am their educator, but they had educated me. After placing my ego aside and consulting with a mentor, she told me that it is our job as teachers to curate learning experiences. We will not know everything because knowing everything is an impossible task. But, we can create experiences for our students that inspire them to think and push boundaries.

Just as I will teach my students, my students will also teach me. I will continue to learn throughout my career, and that is what makes excellent educators.

As you embark through the rest of this chapter, we wanted to make sure you had a clear map of the concepts and ideas that will be explored more in depth. As we mentioned previously in the introduction, do not feel pressured to try and apply all of these ideas, rather explore as many of these as you can and apply what piques your interests or needs. Enjoy exploring the following toolbox tactics:

1. Once in a While, Leave Work at Work: Giving yourself grace and understanding that it is alright to leave the piles of grading, planning, and other work, in your classroom so you can unwind and recharge your batteries.

2. Taking Care of Yourself: You cannot fill the cups of your students if your cup is empty. Taking care of yourself is the most selfless thing you can do for your students.

3. Spend Time Exploring: The community surrounding your school can help tell the story of your students; explore around to learn more about the community you are serving.

4. Incorporate your passions: Incorporating your personal passions can do wonders for bringing your curriculum and standards alive in your classroom.

TOOLKIT TACTIC 2.1 ONCE IN A WHILE, LEAVE WORK AT WORK

Case: *Especially in your first years of teaching, there may be the urge to assess every single thing that your students do in every subject that you teach. There are only so many hours in a day, so this would result in bringing plenty of piles home to continue marking at the dining room table or your home office. How necessary is this? Is this a practice of yours, currently?*

From Vince: *Oh! The amount of times I would bring my work home just for it to live in my bag was incredible! There were times when I would stare at my work bag with an extreme amount of guilt, almost coaxing me into working long hours. While sometimes that is necessary, the guilty feelings are not! Leaving work at work will promote opportunities for a well-deserved break, hopefully without the feelings of guilt!*

SCHOOL STORIES

Mr. Nguyen's Experience

7:15 p.m. "No one told me how much work teaching is," I thought as I opened my car door. I tossed my laptop, planner, messenger bag, uneaten lunch, empty travel mug, and a stack of unmarked English essays in the backseat of my car. Once in the driver's seat, I sat, took a deep breath, and started my commute home. When I got home, it was nearly 8:00 p.m. I placed the contents of my backseat on the kitchen table and sat down, thinking about tonight's hockey game, what to make for dinner, how long it's been since I've been to the gym, and the essays that *still* needed marking. "Report cards aren't due until Friday . . . I still have a few days," I thought, as I opened my uneaten lunch, which turned into dinner. After eating, I sat on my couch, turned on the television to the hockey game, and promptly drifted off to sleep. Startled awake at 1:00 in the morning, I looked at the pile of unmarked essays. "Maybe tomorrow," I said out loud, as I climbed the stairs to continue my sleep. The alarm would go off before I knew it.

The teaching profession never stops; the expectations in this role are high and the time we have to meet those expectations is limited. There are many teachers just like Alex in schools all around the world, hoping to do their best work to serve their students in all 24 hours we are given a day. The reality of teaching is that there will always be assessing, scheduling, grading, cleaning, organizing, planning, decorating, and meeting with colleagues. The bulk of our assignable time is to teach students the curriculum and life skills along the way. What little time is left can be spent on some of the other tasks, but these tasks should not be your identity, nor should they take over your life! You are more than Mr./Mrs./Ms./Mx. ________. In order to be the best we can for our students, we have to take care of ourselves in the best ways we can. That includes keeping work at work! Occasionally, it makes sense to do a little bit of work in the evenings or weekends; however, that should not be the norm. It is okay to leave work at work and enjoy your time in the evenings and on the weekends. The truth is your to-do list will be there tomorrow. You will, inevitably, add to it. Take time to rest, recharge, and rejuvenate, so that you can be the best version of yourself for your students the following day.

BEST PRACTICES

Inevitably, you won't be able to do everything during work hours. It's simply not possible to do everything in the short work hours of each day. If you do have to bring work home with you, here a few tips to consider:

1. *Don't sacrifice sleep*. It's vitally important to be well rested when embarking on a new school day. In order to do so, you need to rest! By getting a full night of sleep, you will be a more effective teacher. If you can, set an actual alarm clock; not your cellphone. Power down half an hour before bed and focus on settling your mind in order to sleep well.
2. *Set a timer.* If you need to work at home, take into consideration how much time you'd like to work. If we send home work for students to do, we often say not to work for no more than 30 minutes, in order to honor their time away from working.

Consider the same for yourself; set a timer for 30 minutes or an hour, maximum. When the timer rings, your time is up!

3. *Be realistic.* Can you get through three piles of grading, creating a new seating plan, and planning for coaching your school's basketball team? Maybe. Is it necessary? Probably not. Be realistic in how much you can get done in an hour after school.
4. *Only bring home what is manageable.* Consider the after-school commitments that you already have, nourishing your body, movement, downtime, and connection with others. Then, ask yourself what is manageable for the time that remains.

EQUITABLE PRACTICES

Wellness can be defined as the state of living a healthy lifestyle. Depending on where you are from, your circumstances, or your ability, your version of wellness may look different from wellness practices that your colleague, sibling, or friend may take part in. Wellness also encompasses balance and the existence of it in your day-to-day practice.

1. *Rest.* You are no good to those that need you if you don't take care of yourself first. Something to keep in mind is that not all adults need a full eight hours of sleep to feel rested.
2. *Reflection.* Take moments to reflect. Reflection can look very diverse. Meditation, smudging, prayer, journaling, voice notes; these are all ways that one can take part in reflective practices.
3. *Pastimes.* Engage in social activities with others. Joining a league sport, music lessons, a crocheting group, baking, fitness classes; the sky's the limit.
4. *Limit screen time.* Especially before going to bed, limit your access to screens, social media, and your computer or laptop.

QUESTIONS TO ASK YOUR MENTOR OR COLLEAGUES

1. What methods or strategies do you use to mitigate burnout with bringing work home?

2. What best practices do you have for keeping work and home separate?
3. Are there any tips or tricks you can share with me to help me maximize my time spent at school so that I can find balance?

REFLECTIVE PRACTICE

Think about how you plan to take care of yourself. Consider setting a timer after school hours and once it rings, it is time to pack up. Perhaps your grade partner or neighboring teacher could be your time accountability partner; make an agreement that you will both be out of the building by 4:30 p.m. each day. Do you eat lunch with your students? You need a break from them, just as they need time away from you. Consider eating in your staffroom once a week to start and increase that number every few weeks. In what ways can you increase your wellness? Is there a hobby or sport you have always wanted to try out? Consider signing up for a sport and social club, or dance class!

SELF-REFLECTION (POST-READING)

What do you like to do for fun?

Has that hobby or activity continued or stopped since the school year began?

In what ways can you keep yourself accountable?

TOOLKIT TACTIC 2.2 TAKING CARE OF YOURSELF

Case: *There are many analogies about taking care of yourself. As someone who loves to travel, the one that resonates with me (Sarah)*

(Continued)

(Continued)

the most is to "put your oxygen mask on before assisting others." In order to be effective in your classroom, it is imperative that you take care of yourself and do what is best for you, mind, body, and soul. Part of your employment as a teacher includes benefits. In many places, teacher benefit packages are fantastic and encompass massages, chiropractors, therapy, dentist visits, prescription medication, and more. The benefits allocated to you are provided to you in order to take care of yourself. Be sure to explore your benefits and see how you can utilize them throughout the year. Taking care of yourself will mean different things to different people. Through this Toolkit Tactic, we will explore what self-care is and areas that we can continue to grow when looking at taking care of yourself.

***From Sarah:** I love this chapter because I find that it's a great reminder for myself, even as someone who is out of the classroom. To take care of oneself looks different to everyone; what my coauthors and friends need is much different than what I require to be a functioning human. Things that I do for myself is listen to audiobooks, bake muffins and pies, take naps, play basketball, and watch Netflix "reality" shows. All of these things, I've learned, are not earned, but required for me to show up as my best self for the people around me. Now it's your turn, what do you do for self-care?*

AUTHOR'S CORNER

Sarah's Experience

For a long time, I taught in a sixth-grade classroom. I was often the first teacher in the building and the last one to leave. I had so many ideas and felt that I needed to execute every single one in order to be the fantastic teacher that my students deserved. As an elementary teacher, I found hands-on learning experiences to be the most effective for my students and, in a world that is continuing to lean in a more digital space, spent a lot of time creating assignments and projects with a digital or STEM component in order to reach all of the learners in my room. Being in the classroom from 7:15 a.m. until 6:00 p.m., often not stopping to eat a proper lunch, go to the bathroom, have a drink of water, or connect with other adults was not at all ideal, but I thought it was necessary. I was running on jujubes and iced coffee and made excuses for my increasingly poor diet and lack of physical activity. Something that my Mom continued to say to me was, "If you don't decide to take a break, your body will tell you when you take a break." Boy, was she right! I found myself getting more and more run-down, fatigued, sore, and sick. Eventually, it got to a point that I couldn't get out of bed without feeling nauseous and dizzy, and I was forced to turn right back around when I entered the school and felt as though I was going to faint. My body was taking the break that I kept dodging and there was nothing I could do about it.

Self-care. We hear all the time, "It's important to take care of yourself," and, "It's important to indulge in self-care."

What is self-care? How do you know when to take care of yourself?

Self-care can be categorized in a few different ways. It is also something that is completely individual. What one person may consider self-care could be torture to another; for example, one of the things I do to take care of myself is book a massage for myself once a month. It helps with my muscles, which are often tight from either sitting too long or not sitting at all. My best friend, on the other hand, can't bear the thought of a full-body massage. The entire notion freaks her out. You have to consider what your body needs to feel good, feel strong, and feel well enough to perform all of your duties as a teacher. Consider the following things when figuring out what is best for you.

EXERCISE

Movement is an important thing that we all require. Exercise and activity is something that we all need in order to keep our bodies from deteriorating. Not everyone is prepared to start their fitness journey with a 10 km run or a HIIT class. Movement is important in whatever form you like. It may seem daunting to try to fit in a group fitness class before or after work, but getting into the habit of some form of movement is very beneficial for your body. Personally, I found that basketball and boxing were two activities that I prioritized after work. Both are fun to do in a group or on your own. Additionally, after 30 minutes, you feel great! If you are someone motivated by a coach or an instructor, group fitness classes or a sport and social club is a great way to, not only connect with others, but to keep your body moving. A solo activity may be more your speed; a walk, swimming laps, an elliptical—there are many options. The most important thing is to start and to be as consistent as possible. I have taken a walk first thing in the morning to start my day, and different fitness classes at my local gym throughout the week for Zumba, spin, and cardio boxing. The most difficult thing is to start, but each time I do, I immediately feel better. Many city facilities have great price points for teachers and evening and early morning options. Find what works best for you. It may take some trial and error, but it is worth it for your overall health, energy, and self-care.

THERAPY AND COUNSELING

As a new teacher, you may feel overwhelmed with the amount of work you're accountable for, assessment, meeting with parents, classroom management, and more; that's just within the walls of the school! Trying to balance a busy work schedule and what could be a busy home life, social life, and personal time with loved ones can spread a person incredibly thin. Therapy is something that used to be overly stigmatized. Society has come a long way in its overall acceptance of and empowerment of going to talk to someone when you need to. Therapy can be used as a form of self-care for your mind and soul. It can be difficult, for some, to discuss a problem with those closest to them. Folks sometimes feel as though they are burdening their family and friends with an issue or problem they may be encountering. Speaking to a licensed therapist, someone that you don't know, can bring a sense of ease. Therapists aren't there to judge; they are there to offer support and advice, as well as to make you think and consider different perspectives or reconsider your own. There is no shame in connecting with a therapist to help you with any hardship you may be experiencing.

FOOD

The way that you nourish your body is very important. It can also be very difficult, depending on the timing of your breaks and lunch at school. Sometimes, in a 15-minute recess break, you have to choose one of a myriad of things, including having a snack. When it comes to food before, during, and after school, there are many things to consider; one of the most crucial being consistency. Fixing a regular and healthy breakfast, lunch, and dinner will help to keep you satiated and satisfied throughout the day. Sometimes the sheer thought of preparing food for three meals a day, five days a week can be daunting. Taking things one step at a time can include preboiling eggs for the week, baking muffins to take as snacks or breakfast, meal-prepping large meals that can be divided, and even pre-preparing smoothie bags, are all a first step that you can take. Setting aside part of one day a week to dedicate to this is a great way to take away the chore of cooking day in and day out. Personally, I choose Sunday afternoons. I will prepare lunches and dinners for the week that are easy to store and freeze. I also eat a lot of fruit and will take the time to wash, cut, and bag fruit so that I can grab it to go on my way to work. Finally, make it fun! My friends will come over each week and we will make an afternoon of making breakfast wraps, lasagna, sandwiches, stir-frys, and other meals that are old favorites or experiment with new recipes. This helps with variety and is a great way to make cooking social. I follow many creators online with plenty of great recipes and food saving tips, which helps me to stay on top of eating good, quality, healthy food, that will keep me full for a longer period of time and will discourage me from using delivery apps to order cheeseburgers and pizza. Every once in a while, it's a treat, but making it a daily occurrence is, for one thing, very expensive, but on the other hand, is quite unhealthy. Ensuring that I am eating healthy food is a part of my self-care. It's the way that I show myself that I care for myself.

REST

Perhaps it's silly to say, but one of my (Sarah) favorite pastimes is napping. I am one of those folks who, while sitting on an airplane, will fall asleep before the flight attendants can tell me my nearest exit. One thing I have learned about myself is that my body requires anywhere between six and a half to eight hours of sleep every night. In knowing this, I am able to work backward to figure out my optimal bedtime in order to maximize my productivity the next day. The amount of sleep I require is average for an adult, but it doesn't always happen. I have learned that saying no to things like constant gatherings and parties is important for my rest. Although I enjoy spending time with others, I also value my own time, solo, away from others in order to rest. Sometimes, taking time to rest means taking a nap. In other instances, it means curling up with a cup of tea and a book, with my phone on "do not disturb." Rest is important, as it allows your body to rejuvenate from a long day, hard work, due to stress, or a plethora of other reasons. Rest when you need to, in whatever way you require.

There are many things that you can do, beyond this list, to prioritize yourself. Self-care is fundamental. What works for you may not work for everyone, and that is okay! Take the time to figure out what you need to be your best self, both in and out of the classroom.

QUESTIONS TO ASK YOUR MENTOR OR COLLEAGUES

When it comes to taking care of yourself, don't be shy! In order for you to be a great teacher, it's important that you're open and honest with yourself and how you feel. If you're wondering about what to ask your mentor, try out some of these questions:

1. Is there a maximum amount of sick days available to me?
2. How do I apply for a leave, should I need one?
3. When can I utilize a personal day?

SELF-REFLECTION (POST-READING)

What do you indulge in when it comes to self-care?

Do you have a routine or ritual for making sure that you take care of yourself?

What do you do when you start to feel sick?

TOOLKIT TACTIC 2.3 SPEND TIME EXPLORING

Case: *As a young teacher, a great way to get to know your community is to explore! Whether you are new to a school or new to a neighborhood, take the time to explore. Involve your students in exploring and allow them to get to know and get comfortable with their community. When it comes to moments after school, connect with other staff members to explore even further and get to know your community on a personal and professional level.*

From Tim: *My first full-time teaching job was in a small rural town of 600 people in northern Alberta. Living over 4000 km (2500 miles) away from where I grew up, I very much felt like a stranger. On evening walks, I would stop by different businesses (corner store, hardware, grocery shop, barber, post office, etc.) as well as community service groups to introduce myself. Soon people knew me by name and I knew them. Invitations to family dinners, or to go golfing and curling became common. I even joined the volunteer fire* *department. In taking the initiative to explore the surrounding community and say hello, I soon felt more connected to my school community which truly helped me to better understand the students I would be teaching.*

GET TO KNOW YOUR COMMUNITY

A wonderful way to get to know your community is to ask! Connect with other teachers, chat with parents, and search for things in your community that peak your interest. Check out museums, local restaurants, public parks, and boutiques. There are many ways to make authentic learning experiences for students with the places in their community. I (Sarah) was teaching Grade 3 the year that a brand new arena was being built in the city. I took that as a curricular field trip opportunity and tied its development to curricular outcomes that I am accountable for. Over three years, my students and I went to the site and spoke with construction workers, did mapping, numeracy, and wrote stories. Then, we would walk through the downtown core and learn about some of the local restaurants, speak to shop owners, and play in the city hall fountains. Those are experiences that we couldn't have had by staying in our classroom. In my quest to make exploration fun for my students, we created challenges and projects based on our city and the people the students met along the way. Many establishments look to offer programs and field trips for students to partake in. As often as possible, connect the curriculum that you are responsible for to real life experiences, places, and people. These are the things that students will remember most.

BUILD YOUR OWN COMMUNITY

You're a person before you are a teacher. Finding connection with others can be intimidating, but a great way to make friends and collaborate. Step away from the school in order to build community. Take the opportunity to build a community among the staff at your school. Join a fitness class together, take in team building opportunities, try out new breweries or cafes, check out farmer's markets, or escape for weekend trips to the mountains. There are many more ways to build community between you and your colleagues, which will strengthen your staff camaraderie. Take some time to get to know the people that you work with and see how you can build community among yourselves in the community that you work in.

RURAL LIVING VS. CITY LIVING

You may find a job in your first few years in a city or town that is far from where you live. You may find a job in a rural area while living in the city, and vice-versa. If you are anything like me, you are a city kid with very little knowledge of a small town or farm. Consider connecting with folks in the surrounding area or other teachers to see where your worlds might collide; perhaps there are land-based learning opportunities that your students can take part in, for example. There is a lot of learning that can be done by tending to a farm or a patch of land. Land-based activities, like anything, can be incredibly cross-curricular. Additionally, utilizing an outdoor classroom is a wonderful way for students to connect with their environment and learn from those that work in a rural setting as well.

QUESTIONS TO ASK YOUR MENTOR OR COLLEAGUES

Consider asking your mentor one of the following questions:

1. How can we incorporate the land to the activities we do in the classroom?
2. In what ways can I create a classroom community for my students?
3. How can I make the community around us an authentic learning experience for students?
4. Is there a way to create a community amongst the staff in our school? What is the best way to do so?

SELF-REFLECTION (POST-READING)

What activities do you like to do with others?

Where do community and curriculum connect?

In what ways can I create an authentic learning experience for students in our school and outside in our community?

TOOLKIT TACTIC 2.4 INCORPORATE YOUR PASSIONS

Case: *Depending on the grade level or subject area that you teach, you may find authentic, real-world connections for students. How can you incorporate the things that you are passionate about for the students you teach?*

From Wayne: *A number of years ago I was able to work with a teacher who embodied the concept of perpetual re-invention. He was not only a great teacher but was also self-taught in airbrushing, electronics, the bass guitar, and a number of other skills. He was not afraid to fail as he learned more and more and was also not afraid to share his many talents and passions with his students. He would play an important role in the rebirth of our school and go on to work with a number of students who needed his passions and commitment to learning. Never be afraid of bringing your passions to school!*

CONSIDER YOUR PASSION

As I have grown as an educator, I (Sarah) have unlocked a strong passion for human rights education, diversity, anti-racism, inclusion, and equity. These things have always been important to me, but many events in the world we live in and the ability for students to see things happen in real time convinced me to bring these things into my teaching. Current events and utilizing social media is a great way to leverage what you might find passion in or what you may find important. I have found that there are nonnegotiables in my teaching, as well. For example, representation is imperative. Students need to see themselves represented in the classroom and the world around them. As educators, we are teaching more and more diverse populations of children. Additionally, the world that our students are currently in will become even more diverse as they grow older. We, as teachers, should look beyond race when it comes to diversity. Students are diverse in the languages they speak, the food they eat, their heights and sizes, their likes and dislikes, their abilities or challenges, the way they learn . . . the list could go on and on. When I considered this in my own classroom, I was bringing in books in multiple languages, books with protagonists that are different sizes, features of cultural food and music, and more. Students who are exposed to diversity and the different lenses and passions of their peers and their teacher will only create a greater classroom culture.

WINDOWS, MIRRORS, AND SLIDING GLASS DOORS

Dr. Rudine Sims Bishop (1990) coined the notion that, in order for students to be more well-rounded learners, not only do we need to include representation, but we need to expose them to the passions and point of view of others. We can do this with an analogy of windows, mirrors, and sliding glass doors. A mirror is a reflection for students—it is representation or how students can see themselves. A window allows them to look into the passion or point of view of someone else. A sliding glass door has the ability to transport students' thoughts and feelings around a topic and perhaps learn empathy or the point of view of another and why they may feel that way.

Here is an example.

Window	Mirror	Sliding Glass Door
Starr lives in a neighborhood and experiences things I haven't because the neighborhood I lived in is the opposite. I wonder . . .	The cover of the book *The Hate U Give* by Angie Thomas features a young Black teen, Starr, that looks a lot like me.	Starr went through a tragic event in the story. Although I have been through sad things, it's not the same as what she went through. If I were her . . .

A book like this one brings more than just representation for young, Black teens. It provides insight into a world that I didn't experience. My passion for representation is fueled by this book and others, and it is such an easy way to allow students to see themselves and make connections for themselves and others.

In this table, list three things you're passionate about and how you can make these passions a part of your classroom.

Passion	Connection

QUESTIONS TO ASK YOUR MENTOR OR COLLEAGUES

Here are some questions to pose to your mentor, when it comes to incorporating the things you are most passionate about:

1. What is the easiest way to connect the things I value to the curriculum?
2. Is there an authentic way to connect the interests of the students to what I am expected to cover?

(Continued)

(Continued)

3. Will I be penalized by using the things I am passionate about to help me teach things like numeracy, literacy, or religious education?

SELF-REFLECTION (POST-READING)

What are you most passionate about?

How can you connect that passion to the curriculum?

Do you have interests or passions in common with others within your classroom?

What is the best way to scaffold your interests to make them palatable for students?

BRINGING IT ALL TOGETHER

VOICES FROM THE FIELD

All About Balance

Caitlyn Sly

In my first year of teaching, I found myself caught in a relentless cycle of long hours, trying to get ahead. I would arrive at school by 6:00 a.m. and often wouldn't leave until at least 7:00 p.m. I added to my workload by volunteering on weekends, coaching teams, running clubs, and joining my local association in whatever little free time I had. At first, this intense effort seemed to pay off—my grading was up to date, my lesson plans were meticulously prepared, and my administration noticed my dedication. I believed that if I worked hard enough, I would eventually "make it" and be able to slow down.

However, I didn't realize then that my approach was unsustainable. When report card season arrived, I found myself buried in government assessments, observations, and extracurricular commitments. There were days I didn't even see sunlight, and I eventually hit a wall. After noticing that I had rarely left the building, my administrator had told me that his goal was for me to learn about a work-life balance. A light had switched on for me. I had realized that I had not seen my friends or even my family for several months and all of my relationships outside of the workplace had suffered.

My colleagues had begun to notice that I was also struggling to find a balance between those I love at home and the career I loved. I knew I needed to make a change, I just didn't know how to go about it. I confided in one of the teachers down the hall from me, and she made it her mission every day when she was leaving to stand in front of my classroom door and ensure that I would pack up my things and go home. For the rest of the year, she and I would walk out of the school together. As time went on, my excessively large bag of school work grew smaller and smaller. I would take less and less home, leaving work at work as much as I could.

By my second year, I had embraced this new perspective. I knew I wouldn't make it through the year if I didn't take care of myself. I realized that tasks I thought needed immediate attention at 9 p.m. could wait until the next morning. I designated Sunday afternoons for planning and continued arriving early since I'm a morning person, but I made it a point to leave in a timely manner after the bell, unless I was coaching. I had learned to lean on my colleagues when I needed help and prioritized my health. I spent more time with friends, family, and colleagues. This balance that I had found ensured that I finished my year successfully. I loved going into work every day, and I cherished my time with my loved ones at home. Finding the balance kept me from burning out of my career and ensuring I can continue to do the job that I love.

In many ways, it is easy to overlook well-being and self-care. Especially in your first few years, it is easy to prioritize classroom decor, assessing every piece of work students complete, supervision, and lesson planning. Taking care of all aspects of your whole self will subsequently strengthen your skills as a teacher. When looking to create community, do so both in and out of the classroom, with students and colleagues alike. There are many benefits to this for your school community. Consider things like movement, meditation, rest, and meal prepping. Anything that will nourish your mind, body, and soul, are things that should take priority for you. Your students will pick up on the things that bring you joy and the things that you are passionate about and how they come together and connect to the curriculum. Don't be ashamed to incorporate things that are special to you in the teaching you provide. After all, you have to put your oxygen mask on before assisting someone else. In order to be the best teacher you can be, you have to take care of yourself so you can take care of others.

The implementation tracker included on the next two pages can serve as a tool to measure how well you are incorporating self-care into your busy routine. It is not selfish to take care of yourself, and we hope you engage with this tool frequently. You are working hard, and you deserve the opportunity to take care of your physical, mental, emotional, and social well-being.

IMPLEMENTATION TRACKER

Attempted toolbox tactic:	
Successes:	Roadblocks:
What should I change to be more successful next time?	

<table>
<tr><td colspan="2">Attempted toolbox tactic:</td></tr>
<tr><td>Successes:</td><td>Roadblocks:</td></tr>
<tr><td colspan="2">What should I change to be more successful next time?</td></tr>
</table>

3

THE FIRST DAYS: FIGURING OUT YOUR NEW SCHOOL

As a new teacher stepping into the classroom for the first time, the initial days can be met with a mixture of excitement, anticipation, and perhaps a hint of nervousness. You're not just entering a physical space; you're entering a community of learners, each with their own stories, experiences, and needs. In these foundational days, one of the most crucial tasks is to get to know your people—the standards, codes of conduct, students, colleagues, and administrators—who will become integral parts of your teaching journey.

KNOWING YOUR STANDARDS

Understanding the academic standards relevant to your subject and grade level is essential for effective lesson planning and instruction. Familiarize yourself with the curriculum frameworks, state standards, or national guidelines that outline the knowledge and skills students are expected to acquire. This knowledge serves as a roadmap for designing meaningful learning experiences and assessing student progress. By aligning your teaching practices with established standards, you ensure that your instruction is purposeful, coherent, and targeted toward meeting the needs of your students.

KNOWING YOUR CODES OF CONDUCT

Establishing a positive classroom culture begins with clear expectations for behavior and conduct. Familiarize yourself with the school's codes of conduct, discipline policies, and expectations for student behavior. Communicate these guidelines to your students in a clear and consistent manner, emphasizing the importance of respect, responsibility, and accountability in creating a safe and inclusive learning environment.

Educator and author Harry K. Wong (2018), in his book *The First Days of School*, underscores the significance of setting clear expectations and routines from the outset. By establishing a structured and supportive classroom environment, you create a foundation for academic success and positive social interactions. Consistent enforcement of rules and consequences helps maintain a sense of order and fairness, fostering a conducive learning environment for all students.

TAKING CARE OF YOURSELF

Amid the excitement and challenges of your new role, it's essential to prioritize self-care. Teaching can be demanding both mentally and emotionally, and neglecting your well-being can lead to burnout. Make time for activities that nourish your mind, body, and spirit, whether it's exercise, meditation, hobbies, or spending time with loved ones. Remember that you can't pour from an empty cup, and by taking care of yourself, you'll be better equipped to support your students and colleagues.

COLLABORATING WITH COLLEAGUES AND BUILDING RELATIONSHIPS WITH ADMINISTRATORS

Teaching is not a solitary endeavor; it thrives on collaboration and teamwork. Your colleagues—fellow teachers, support staff, and administrators—are valuable resources who can offer guidance, support, and mentorship as you navigate the challenges and triumphs of your first days in the classroom. Take advantage of opportunities to observe experienced educators in action, participate in professional development workshops, and engage in collaborative planning sessions.

Administrators play a pivotal role in shaping the educational landscape of your school. Establishing positive relationships with administrators from the outset sets the stage for open communication, mutual respect, and professional growth. Seek opportunities to meet with your administrators, share your goals and aspirations, and solicit feedback on your teaching practice.

In his book *The Principal: Three Keys to Maximizing Impact*, author Michael Fullan emphasizes the importance of distributed leadership in fostering a culture of collaboration and continuous improvement. By forging strong partnerships with your administrators, you contribute to a supportive and cohesive school community where all stakeholders are invested in the success of every student.

The first days as a new teacher are a time of exploration, discovery, and relationship building. By getting to know your people you lay the groundwork for a fulfilling and impactful school year and teaching career! Remember to approach each interaction with empathy, curiosity, and a willingness to learn, and embrace the journey ahead with enthusiasm and determination. It is our hope that the following building blocks will provide some inspiration and ways for you to become more comfortable as you embark on your teaching journey!

The early days and months of teaching are somewhat akin to sightseeing at 200 miles an hour. You are trying to take it all in, learn from the inevitable missteps we all make, fit in with your new colleagues, answer the bell each morning and be the best teacher you can be. No doubt your school leader and mentor teacher (if you have one) will be suggesting or outright asking you to take on pursuits beyond the walls of your learning space, coaching, directing the musical, editing the yearbook, or looking after the chess club. You will also have family and friends calling and asking how things are going and seeing if you are available for dinner on Sunday night or to go for wings on Thursday. At some point, all of this may have you feeling a bit overwhelmed or at least fraying at the edges.

Thus, learning how to prioritize is a necessary skill you will need to develop. Visualize all these competing interests like items to be packed in a suitcase. To fit it all in requires thoughtful organization, strategic planning, and a focus on essentials to ensure everything fits and functions together. Here's how this metaphor translates into practical strategies for managing your workload, family, and friends and other priorities. And because emergencies and the unexpected will occur, teachers should remain flexible in their approach. This includes adjusting lesson plans based on student needs, embracing new teaching methodologies, and incorporating feedback for continuous improvement. Thus leaving a little extra space in your suitcase is always a good idea!

As you embark through the rest of this chapter, we wanted to make sure you had a clear map of the concepts and ideas that will be explored more in depth. As we mentioned previously in the introduction, do not feel pressured to try and apply all of these ideas, rather explore as many of these as you can and apply what piques your interests or needs. Enjoy exploring the following toolbox tactics:

1. Getting to Know Your School and School District: Learning more about the school where you are working such as location, commute length, and policies and procedures will help you settle into your teaching role more seamlessly.
2. Getting to Know Your Code of Conduct: The common language in which all teaching and learning policy is created. Take time to familiarize yourself with your code of conduct.
3. Getting to Know Your People: Your school has key individuals beyond the students, teachers, and leaders. Make sure you authentically connect with every member in your school community.
4. Getting to Know Your Mentor or Cooperating Teacher: Whether formal or informal, mentors and colleagues will be there alongside you for your first few years. Find the person or people that will be your constant support and copilot through your school year.

TOOLKIT TACTIC 3.1 GETTING TO KNOW YOUR SCHOOL AND SCHOOL DISTRICT

Case: *Starting a new job in a potentially new city can be overwhelming! There are some steps you can take even before stepping into your classroom for the first time that will help mitigate some of the stressors of starting a new school year. Being deliberate in learning about your school and district will help ease the transition into a wonderful school year.*

From Vince: *I remember moving to my new community and not knowing much about navigating a place that was ten times more populated than where I grew up. Knowing and having multiple routes to get me to school saved me from bad traffic, worse weather, and the never ending* *road construction that would throw a wrench into my commute plans weekly. Taking time to learn about my new school allowed me to not have to worry about the small things, making me a better teacher in the classroom.*

Embarking on your journey as a new teacher or student teacher involves more than just mastering lesson plans and classroom management techniques. It also requires immersing yourself in the rich tapestry of your school and district community. In many ways, doing some early research about your school and school district helps to mitigate some of the stresses of the first few days. We compiled a list of some of the considerations and recommendations we feel are important as you get to know about your school and school district.

FAMILIARIZE YOURSELF WITH THE LOCATION OF THE SCHOOL

This may sound a bit ridiculous, but take some time to understand where your school is located in relation to your commute, as well as amenities around the school. Sounds obvious right? But trust us, there is nothing worse than not having a backup plan of how to get to school on time if there is traffic, road construction, or even inclement weather. Having a planned route and an alternate route will save you some time randomly searching through your maps program in the morning, or even being victimized by heavy traffic or in the case of us writing the book, a freak snow storm! We cannot emphasize how important this is especially if you are not only new to a school, but also have moved to a new city for your job. For those of you who are morning drive-thru coffee (or breakfast) people, it may also be of benefit to you to learn where those are located along the way as well. Taking a few extra minutes in the morning to get your coffee from your favorite on-the-way coffee shop will result in a much smoother start to the day, versus being late with a coffee cup in your hands!

Knowing more about the neighborhood around your school will help you for a few reasons. Firstly, many of us may not teach in the same neighborhood where we live and as such it is important to understand the neighborhood community that your school serves. Being sensitive to the cultural and ethnic demographics of your neighborhood is vital to learning about the students in your classroom and providing you an opportunity to embrace, and celebrate their cultures. Having knowledge of the unique neighborhood you serve will also improve your ability to connect with the families of the students you teach. Supporting local businesses, eating in neighborhood restaurants, and even going to community events, will give you a chance to bump into parents and students and just say hello, and get to know you a bit more out of the classroom context. Let's look at Gamesh Patel's experience.

SCHOOL STORIES

Gamesh Patel, the newest teacher at Mountainview High School, stood in the hallway between classes on Monday morning, chatting with his mentor, Lucy. The bustling corridor was filling quickly with students moving to their next period, their laughter and chatter creating a lively atmosphere.

"So, two months into a new school, a new town, and definitely a new climate. How's it going?" Lucy asked, her tone warm and encouraging.

"It's been a lot to take in, but I'm enjoying it," Gamesh replied. "Still trying to get to know everyone and find my place. Bought my first pair of winter boots Saturday!"

Just then, a group of students approached them, their faces lighting up as they saw Gamesh.

"Mr. Patel!" Jenny called out. "You came to our hockey game! It was so cool to see you there."

Another student chimed in, "You almost got hit when Sonya's slapshot got deflected into the stands! I heard Cindy's grandma gave you the puck!"

Gamesh smiled, genuinely touched by their appreciation. "I had a great time. You all played really well. And yes, getting the puck was a thrill but seeing Letitia get a goal was pretty terrific too!"

After a few more words of thanks, the students waved goodbye and hurried off to their classes. Gamesh turned to Lucy, his smile turning a bit sheepish.

"Lucy, I have to admit something," he said. "I don't know anything about hockey. I don't understand the rules at all. I've never even been on ice before."

Lucy laughed. "Doesn't matter. I had at least half a dozen parents send me a text that you were there. They were genuinely impressed to see you there."

Gamesh laughed. "I heard the students talking about the game all week, and after your suggestion that I learn more about the things that are important to them, I decided to go. It was so fast! And rough!"

Lucy nodded approvingly. "That's a great attitude, Gamesh. The students notice when teachers show interest in their lives outside of school. It makes them feel valued and supported."

"I could tell it meant a lot to them," Gamesh said thoughtfully. "Even if I didn't understand what was happening on the ice, it was fun to be there watching them."

"It absolutely was," Lucy agreed. "And don't worry about the rules. You'll pick them up over time. What matters most is that you're trying to connect with the students and learn about the community. By the way, Jenny's dad told me he has a jersey for you to wear at the next game if you want it."

Gamesh felt a renewed sense of purpose and belonging. "Thanks, Lucy. I'm looking forward to getting more involved. Maybe next time, I'll even learn what icing is."

Lucy laughed. "One step at a time, Gamesh. One step at a time."

FAMILIARIZE YOURSELF WITH POLICIES AND PROCEDURES

Each school and district operates under its own set of policies, procedures, and protocols. Take the time to familiarize yourself with important documents such as the employee handbook, code of conduct, and emergency response plans. Understanding these guidelines not only ensures your compliance with school regulations but also equips you to navigate various scenarios with confidence and professionalism. If you are a teacher who has come from a different career or school district, this is equally important. Not all policies and procedures are the same and thus we need to ensure we are up to date with the current documents as to ensure we don't fall into the trap of thinking we know best.

- Pay particular attention to policies related to student discipline, special education services, and safety protocols.
- Familiarize yourself with the procedures for handling incidents such as student misconduct, medical emergencies, and campus lockdowns.
- Understand the school's disciplinary policies and procedures for handling student behavior. This includes knowing the steps for addressing minor infractions, major infractions, and the protocols for involving parents, counselors, or administrators.
- Familiarize yourself with the school's code of conduct and the consequences for various types of behavior.

- Know the policies regarding student attendance and absences. This includes the procedures for reporting student absences, handling tardiness, and the requirements for excused and unexcused absences.
- Learn about the grading policies and assessment methods used in your new school and district. This includes understanding the grading scale, how grades are recorded and reported, and the expectations for formative and summative assessments. Be aware of any policies regarding late work, make-up assignments, and grade appeals.
- Familiarize yourself with the policies and procedures for supporting students with special needs. This includes understanding the process for developing and implementing individualized education programs (IEPs), as well as knowing your responsibilities in providing accommodations and modifications for these students.

EMBRACE CURIOSITY

Most importantly it is okay to feel anxious about your role as a new teacher, this is a completely normal feeling. We challenge you to take these feelings and turn them into curiosity, and excitement! Sure there are aspects of the role that will be daunting, but it is equally important to give yourself the opportunity to be proud and of course curious about your new role. Teaching is such a wonderfully fulfilling profession, and sometimes all it takes is for us to step back and appreciate where we are. Approach your new environment with an insatiable curiosity that rivals even the most inquisitive of students. Take the time to explore every nook and cranny of the school building, from the bustling hallways to the quiet corners of the library. Observe the interactions between students and teachers, the dynamics of various classrooms, and the unique quirks that make your school special.

Find places that you love in your school, and make sure you explore those spaces often. For me (Vince) it was the drama room. Keep in mind I am not artistically minded at all, but thankfully for me I was able to befriend an amazing drama teacher named Vern Slipetz. The drama room became a place where I was able to see students in a completely different light and provided me an opportunity to comfortably get out of my comfort zone, seeing as though I was more of an athlete and not a drama person growing up. Anytime I needed a "break" from the walls of my classroom, I would head there on my breaks to chat with Vern or watch his drama productions. It was a needed sanctuary from the stresses of my classroom, and a place within the school I was always welcome.

As you wander through the halls, don't hesitate to strike up conversations with fellow educators and staff members. Each interaction is an opportunity to glean valuable insights into the school's culture, values, and traditions. Whether you're chatting with a veteran teacher in the faculty lounge or sharing a laugh with the custodian during lunch break, every connection strengthens your bond with the school community.

Overall, the school where you work needs to be a place where you feel comfortable, both with the policies and procedures as well as the building and community itself. As a new person coming into a school, you are expected to fall into the routines that have been already established for you. It is important for you to take time to make meaning of these things for yourself, rather than thinking you might understand. Here are some questions you may want to ask your mentor as you take the time to learn more about your school.

QUESTIONS TO ASK YOUR MENTOR OR COLLEAGUES

1. What is a place in the school you like to visit to take a break from your classroom? Why?
2. What do you think are the most important policies and procedures I should know regarding our school?
3. Are there policies and procedures that are more strictly enforced by our administrators?
4. In terms of routines that are established in the school already, which should I attest to immediately to help with my transition into my new role?

TOOLKIT TACTIC 3.2 GETTING TO KNOW YOUR CODE OF CONDUCT

Case: *Getting to know your code of conduct is essential to deepening your understanding of the professional responsibilities of teaching. A code of conduct is a set of guidelines and standards designed to ensure that educators maintain professional behavior and uphold ethical*

(Continued)

(Continued)

practices in their interactions with students, colleagues, and the community. As a legal framework, the policy sets forth the ethical and moral areas of accountability and responsibility that each teacher must embrace. Knowing the specific expectations of your code will help you develop respectful interactions and establish professional boundaries central to being a professional teacher.

From Tim: *I'll admit it: I do not always read the terms and conditions of every new app I download on my device (gasp). I know I should but . . . I just trust and hope that it will all work out. This is not a good strategy at all, however when it comes to legal obligations and responsibilities. Simply stated, we need to know the rules and expectations associated with being a teacher. As professionals we are bound by codes of conduct, policy, and procedure that are meant to inform, guide, and* ***protect us*** *in fulfilling our duties. While not always fun or glamorous in the scope of what we do as teachers, reading and knowing the "rules" are essential!*

SELF-REFLECTION (PRE-READING)

How do you currently understand the expectations described in your district's Code of Conduct policy? What might be two or three key areas to focus on first?

PROFESSIONAL CONDUCT AND EXPECTATIONS

Being aware of the expectations for professional conduct and behavior as a teacher is essential to your growth and success. This includes understanding the policies on professional dress, communication with students and parents, use of social media, and maintaining professional boundaries. Additionally, knowing the procedures for reporting incidents of bullying, harassment, or other concerns involving students or staff, are common elements of existing codes. Why is reviewing your code of conduct so important? As is the case with student learning, we need to know what is expected of us. We can think of the areas set forth in the code as our success criteria. From our experience we know full well that new teachers face several challenges that can lead to their termination. Here are five common reasons:

ACADEMIC DISHONESTY

Manipulating student grades or falsifying academic records undermines the integrity of the educational system and can result in a teacher being fired. Ethical conduct in assessing and reporting student performance is crucial.

DISCRIMINATION OR HARASSMENT

Engaging in discriminatory practices or harassment based on race, gender, or other protected characteristics can lead to termination. Schools are committed to providing an inclusive and safe environment for all students and staff.

INAPPROPRIATE RELATIONSHIPS

Engaging in inappropriate relationships with students is a severe breach of trust and professional ethics, often leading to immediate termination and potential legal consequences.

INCOMPETENCE

Teachers are expected to demonstrate proficiency in their subject matter and classroom management. Inability to effectively teach or manage a classroom can lead to termination, especially if remedial measures fail to show improvement.

VIOLATION OF SCHOOL POLICIES

Failing to adhere to school policies, such as those concerning social media use or maintaining professional boundaries, can result in dismissal. Schools uphold strict policies to maintain their reputation and ensure a safe environment for students.

Let's read a story that offers great advice on how you, as a new teacher, can engage with your district's code of conduct legislation.

SCHOOL STORIES

Unpacking your Code of Professional Conduct

Darcy Jones was thrilled as she stepped into her new classroom at Riverview Junior High. The bright, colorful space, still smelling faintly

(Continued)

(Continued)

of fresh paint, was a blank canvas for the beginning of her teaching career. As a fresh-faced junior high teacher, she had brimming enthusiasm but knew she needed guidance to navigate her new role effectively. She was particularly anxious however, about the Code of Professional Conduct that was part of her welcome package of materials to review before the first staff meeting. She decided to ask her mentor teacher about it in advance of the staff meeting.

Her mentor, Paulina Gomez, was a seasoned teacher known for her dedication and calm demeanor. Paulina was both admired and respected by her colleagues and students alike, making her the perfect person for Darcy to turn to.

On their first official meeting, Paulina greeted Darcy with a warm smile. "Welcome, Darcy! I'm so glad you're here. Let's talk about some essentials to get you started."

Darcy was eager to absorb as much knowledge as possible. "I am reading through the district's Code of Conduct and am wondering about Section 2.1 of our code that speaks about the importance of maintaining professional relationships. There is so much to take in and reading all of the required expectations feels a bit overwhelming at times. I'd really appreciate any advice you can give me on interacting with students, developing collegial relationships, and communicating with parents and other stakeholders."

Paulina nodded thoughtfully. "Great questions. I know that sometimes digging into policy and procedures can seem daunting for new teachers. One approach I use is to look at each of the criteria found in our code of conduct and create a list of what skills I need to develop and the actions that stem from those skills. Think of it as breaking each concept into bite-size pieces. Let's break it down. First, let's talk about interacting with students. Building trust and respect is key. Remember, middle schoolers are at a stage where they're figuring out who they are. They need to know you care about them beyond just academic achievements. Show interest in their hobbies, listen to their concerns, and be consistent in your expectations and discipline."

Darcy furrowed her brow slightly. "How do I balance being approachable with maintaining my professional authority?"

Paulina smiled. "It's all about finding that sweet spot. Be friendly and approachable, but also set clear boundaries. Consistency is crucial. If you say you'll do something, make sure you follow through. Students appreciate fairness and reliability."

Darcy nodded, jotting down notes. "And what about developing relationships with other teachers and staff?"

"Ah, collegial relationships," Paulina said, leaning back in her chair. "Build strong relationships by being supportive and open. Offer help when you can, and don't be afraid to ask for advice. Attend faculty meetings and social events. It helps to be visible and involved. People appreciate a positive attitude and a willingness to collaborate."

Darcy grinned. "That sounds manageable. And how about communicating with parents and other stakeholders?"

Paulina's expression turned serious. "Effective communication with parents and stakeholders is crucial. Keep them informed about their children's progress and any issues that arise. Be honest but tactful. It's also important to listen to their concerns and work together to address any issues. Regular updates, whether through newsletters, emails, or phone calls, can help build a good rapport."

Darcy looked thoughtful. "What if there's a difficult conversation to be had?"

Paulina's gaze was steady. "Prepare for the conversation by gathering facts and thinking through possible solutions. Approach the conversation with empathy and a problem-solving mindset. Be clear about the issues, and work toward finding a solution together. Even when the conversation is tough, maintaining respect and professionalism is key."

Darcy took a deep breath, feeling a mix of excitement and nervousness. "Thank you, Paulina. This is incredibly helpful. I feel a lot more confident about starting."

Paulina gave her a reassuring smile. "You're going to do great, Darcy. Remember, every teacher has their own style. The Code of Conduct is a helpful guide and it takes time and effort to really unpack and embrace them. Trust yourself and adapt as you learn what works best for you and your students. And always feel free to reach out if you need support."

As Darcy prepared for her first day, she felt a renewed sense of readiness. Thankful for Paulina's guidance to work through each of the polices a little bit at a time, Darcy felt better equipped to engage in the joys and challenges ahead. As she reflected on the meeting with Paulina, she breathed a little easier through her first day jitters, appreciating and understanding that the code of conduct policies and procedures provide an important foundation for her teaching practice and are much more than a set of rules.

Having just read the interaction between Darcy and Paulina, what are two aha moments you found helpful and what is one "I still wonder about" item that you feel you need to learn more about?

Spending time with a mentor teacher to review and discuss local code of conduct legislation, including the proper procedures for how to report violations of the code, is a good way to deepen understanding of these areas. Ultimately, through a focus on the three bullets listed below, new teachers can more readily embrace how to engage with their practice standards and code of conduct.

- **Interactions with Students:** Maintain a professional and respectful relationship with students, avoiding any form of favoritism or inappropriate behavior.
- **Collegial Relationships:** Work collaboratively with colleagues, showing respect and support.
- **Communication:** Communicate effectively and professionally with students, parents, and colleagues.

COMMON ERRORS: SOCIAL MEDIA

In an effort to be relatable or keep up with students, we may make mistakes in approaches to connect with students. One of the errors I (Sarah) made in my early years of teaching was in the world of social media. I was excited to be one of the younger, more tech-savvy teachers on staff and quickly took over the school's social media accounts, as well as created my own for my students. I didn't take into consideration things like photo releases or oversharing things like real-time field trip locations or student achievements. In hindsight, I was a very eager and proud teacher in all of our school's accomplishments, but what I didn't take into account is that social media is a very public entity in society. By posting a tweet like, "Grade 3B is loving the #EdmontonValleyZoo right now! 9/30/2013," I am giving anyone and everyone access to my students and their whereabouts. What's worse, is I was the photo queen with the students in our school. I took photos at after school practices, concerts, field trips, in the hallways, sporting activities, celebrations—you name it, I was there taking photos and posting them in real time. I am very lucky that this was never used inappropriately, but I realized in my fifth year how dangerous it is to do so. Without permission, I was telling the world all about our school and the vulnerable population within it: the children.

From then on, I was sparse with posting and covered up faces with emojis. Parents were thrilled to see their students engaging in so many wonderful opportunities, but ultimately, it became a safety risk to be so public. As a solution, I would take photos and share them with my colleagues, who could then share photos of their students with the parents in their class. It took away the fear and panic that arose thinking of the dangers that are online. Something I teach my students at the start of every year is digital citizenship and their digital footprint. How ironic that it took me so long to learn my own lesson, all in the name of being relatable!

WHAT TO DO V. WHAT NOT TO DO

✔ *Do . . .*	✖ *Do Not . . .*
Talk to students; find out what they like.	Make assumptions based on stereotypes.
Use the internet appropriately.	Use websites like Discord, Reddit, etc. with students.
Take photos; It's wonderful for documenting fun times and growth.	Post photos on your personal social media accounts.
Encourage students to use the internet positively to share the things they learn, and to practice consent if they happen to post about their friends.	Add students to be your friend on social media—that crosses a line that is necessary between a teacher and a student.

Getting to know your school and school district is an essential step in becoming an effective and successful teacher. By embracing curiosity, connecting with colleagues, familiarizing yourself with policies and procedures, engaging with the community, and seeking support when needed, you'll lay the groundwork for a rewarding career in education. Remember, your journey as an educator is just beginning—embrace the challenges, cherish the moments of triumph, and never stop learning and growing along the way.

SELF-REFLECTION (POST-READING)

How can you best relate to the students you serve?

In what creative way can you invite students to connect with you without crossing any boundaries?

QUESTIONS TO ASK YOUR MENTOR OR COLLEAGUES

When considering connection with students, it's really important to ask your mentor about ways that they connect with students. Relationship building is key to connection, but we must do so in an appropriate manner.

1. Are there things or routines that the school already does regarding connection?
2. What does connection look like amongst the students?
3. Do buddy systems exist, and if so, how do they get established?

TOOLKIT TACTIC 3.3 GETTING TO KNOW YOUR PEOPLE

Case: *Establishing effective relationships with students, colleagues, parents, and community members is one of the most important aspects of being an effective teacher. Getting to know who you are serving and supporting is central to fostering such relationships. This involves creating a positive and trusting relationship with students. Building rapport includes engaging with students in a friendly and approachable manner, showing genuine interest in their lives, and acknowledging their individual strengths and challenges. Simple actions like learning students' names quickly, using icebreakers, and engaging in casual conversations can help establish a connection. Creating a welcoming atmosphere where students, colleagues, parents and community members feel comfortable sharing about themselves and their interests can enhance success in knowing your learning community and building positive relationships.*

From Wayne: *I gave up on the gold retirement watch from one school district very early in my career when I decided that there were more adventures to live if I moved from time to time. Thus, I had to get good at being the "new teacher" and getting to know students, staff. I learned to make the first move, to put my hand out first, say hello, ask questions, take direction and get to know my new context. A big part of that was relaxing and enjoying the experience of being new, making a good first impression and being comfortable with change!*

YOU ARE NOT ALONE

Sometimes teaching can ironically feel like a very lonely profession. What we mean by this is that although you are always in a room full of students, it becomes difficult to take time to chat and connect with colleagues. Teaching is a social endeavor, and there will be some days where the students will require all of your social attention to the extent that you may even find yourself eating lunch in the classroom. In order to reenergize your social battery, it is important you connect with some of your colleagues in the school. These can be (but are not limited to) teachers in your grade level, or content area. Some of your best lifelong friendships will be made between you and your colleagues, after all you will be spending a lot of time together over the course of the school year. Thus, do not be afraid to invest time getting to know your colleagues, no matter what position they hold in your school—teacher, office admin, custodian, educational assistant, school leader, whatever. You are all teammates making things better for the students!

We understand the overwhelming feelings that come with starting a new career in a new school, and some days the last thing you may want to do is put yourself out there as the "new person." So we thought we would provide some general suggestions of things you could do as you seek to learn more about your people, and simultaneously have them learn more about the awesome person you are as well!

INTRODUCE YOURSELF

Take the initiative to introduce yourself to colleagues, administrators, and support staff. A brief, friendly introduction can go a long way in making a good first impression.

ATTEND SCHOOL EVENTS AND MEETINGS

Participate in staff meetings, professional development sessions, and social events. This will give you opportunities to meet and interact with colleagues in a more relaxed setting.

JOIN COMMITTEES AND TEAMS

Volunteer for school committees, extracurricular activities, or teams. Working together on common goals fosters collaboration and helps you get to know your colleagues better.

VISIT COMMON AREAS

Spend time in common areas like the teachers' lounge, cafeteria, or workrooms. These are natural settings for casual conversations and relationship building.

ORGANIZE OR ATTEND INFORMAL GATHERINGS

Organize or join informal gatherings, such as coffee breaks, lunch groups, or after-school outings. These settings can provide relaxed opportunities to chat and connect with colleagues who share similar interests to you.

SHARE RESOURCES AND IDEAS

Collaborate with colleagues by sharing teaching resources, lesson plans, or classroom management tips. This not only helps build relationships but also shows that you are a team player.

SET UP ONE-ON-ONE MEETINGS

Arrange short one-on-one meetings or informal chats with key people like your department head, mentor, or administrators. Use these opportunities to learn about their roles and how you can work together effectively.

While this is just a list of the many general actions you can take to get to know your people, please keep a few things in mind when learning about your colleagues. Firstly, remember that many teachers have different levels of comfort when they engage in personal conversations at work. Not all teachers will be willing to talk about social activities, and thus don't be too discouraged if some of your colleagues are a bit less friendly than you had hoped. Secondly, the staffroom can be a great place to unwind and have personal conversations with colleagues; however, in some schools this is also a place that is used to gossip about students (which ones are the "good" students, or "bad" students). We want to caution you away from this harmful practice. Each student has their own independent relationship with their teachers, and a student that one teacher may find challenging another may find the opposite. Do not let the gossip about students influence your existing perception of them, and furthermore bias you into labeling a student.

When we zoom into the daily functions of a school, there is no doubt the impact that all members of the community have on our students. Often, there are groups of unsung heroes who often get overlooked as students start filling our classrooms, and teachers start teaching their lessons. Part of getting to know your people, is also getting to know the people who support you as you teach. After all, without the support staff, our schools would cease to function properly. Here are a few groups of people you definitely need to get to know, along with some ways to get to know them.

Educational Assistants

1. **Collaborative Planning:** Work closely with educational assistants in planning and implementing classroom activities. Share your plans and listen to their insights and suggestions.
2. **Acknowledge Their Contributions:** Regularly acknowledge and appreciate their efforts in supporting students and the classroom. This fosters mutual respect and teamwork.
3. **Professional Development:** Participate in or organize joint professional development sessions. Learning together can strengthen your working relationship.

Custodians

1. **Build Personal Connections:** Take time to introduce yourself and learn their names. Engage in small talk and show genuine interest in their work and well-being. This goes a long way in building positive relationships.
2. **Show Appreciation:** Acknowledge their hard work regularly, whether through simple thank-you notes or verbal appreciation. Occasionally leave a card, or small token of appreciation to let them know how much you appreciate them.
3. **Include Them in the School Community:** Ensure they feel included in the school community by inviting them to school events and treating them as integral members of the team.

Front Office Staff

1. **Introduce Yourself Early:** Make a point to introduce yourself to the front office staff early on. They can be invaluable allies in navigating the school's administrative processes.
2. **Maintain Open Communication:** Keep them informed about your classroom needs and any upcoming events. Clear communication helps them support you more effectively.
3. **Express Gratitude:** Regularly express your gratitude for their help. Small gestures of appreciation can foster a supportive and cooperative relationship.

We cannot stress enough the importance of getting to know and establishing relationships with your school's support staff. As mentioned these unsung heroes are often the secret to a well-functioning school, and without them our jobs as teachers would be exponentially more difficult. Taking a few minutes every week to share a coffee or tea, and engage in a conversation will go a long way as you navigate your way through the school year. If you have certain support staff who have served the school for many years, make sure to ask them about the history of the school as well. You will be surprised at what you learn.

It is also important to get to know the teaching and administration staff at your school beyond the official "Welcome to School" events. Many of these people have your best interests at heart, and will often have the answers to a lot of your questions. Here are some other ways to get to know your colleagues.

Other Teachers

1. **Attend Staff Meetings and Social Events**: Participate actively in staff meetings, professional development sessions, and any social gatherings. This shows your willingness to be part of the team and provides opportunities for informal conversations.
2. **Join Committees and Groups**: Volunteer for school committees or extracurricular activities. Working together on common goals can build strong professional relationships.
3. **Mentorship**: Seek out a mentor or offer to mentor others if you have more experience. This structured relationship can provide ongoing support and collaboration.

Principal

1. **Schedule Regular Check-Ins**: Arrange short, regular meetings with your principal to discuss your progress, ask questions, and seek advice. This shows your commitment and keeps you on their radar.
2. **Engage in Open-Door Policies**: Take advantage of any open-door policies. Approach your principal with ideas, concerns, or just to share updates on your work.
3. **Involve in Decision-Making**: Participate in schoolwide initiatives and offer your input. Showing your investment in the school's success can help build a positive relationship.

Other School Administrators

1. **Be Proactive in Communication**: Introduce yourself and maintain regular communication with vice-principals, department heads, and other administrators. Keep them informed of your classroom activities and any needs you may have.
2. **Seek Feedback and Support**: Request feedback on your performance and ask for support or resources to improve your teaching. This shows you value their input and are keen on professional growth.
3. **Attend Administrative Meetings**: If possible, attend meetings where administrators discuss policies and procedures. This helps you understand their priorities and align your work accordingly.

By implementing these strategies, you'll build strong, positive relationships with all key people in your school, creating a supportive and collaborative environment conducive to your success as a new teacher.

MAKING CONNECTIONS: A CHALLENGE

Use the following table to track your new connections. The challenge is to connect with different school colleagues, not just other teachers! Take a minute to have a conversation and learn something new about them. Simultaneously share something about yourself. Track your new connections in the table.

Who	New Learning About My Colleague
Ex.: Les the custodian	*Ex.: Les immigrated to our country and was a jeweler in his home country of Poland. He still creates new jewelry part-time at his friend's shop.*
______________________ ______________________ ______________________ ______________________	______________________ ______________________ ______________________ ______________________

(Continued)

(Continued)

Who	New Learning About My Colleague

TOOLKIT TACTIC 3.4 GETTING TO KNOW YOUR COOPERATING/MENTOR TEACHER

Case: *When you hear the word mentor you probably think of several other words like guide, coach, or even supervisor. One important thing we want you to keep in mind is that a mentor, whether formally or informally assigned to you, can help you with those early days, weeks, and months of getting familiarized with your new learning community. We know that mentorship normally takes place over a longer period of time whereas coaching takes place in a shorter time frame.*

From Sarah: *I remember student-teaching like it was yesterday. Both times, I worked with mentor teachers who were incredibly inviting, warm, and knowledgeable in all things Grade 2 and Grade 4. My first mentor teacher (Hi, Gina!) showed me how to teach with compassion and patience, how to job-share effectively, and the importance of keeping a decent pair of running shoes under your desk. My second mentor teachers (Hi, Kerri and Gary!) taught me the true meaning of differentiated instruction, how to go with the flow, classroom management in some of the most extreme situations, and how to show love* *to the kids that need it the most. My advice to you is to soak up every moment with your mentor teachers. They're brilliant people.*

As a new member of your school, you are going to build new relationships over time and get to know the existing staff. You might be assigned to a veteran teacher who will serve as your mentor or grade partner. Ideally, this connection will provide you with a *more experienced other* (MEO). This teacher will get to know you and support your growth over the course of your first few formative years as an early career teacher. Often, the MEO that you are partnered with might be someone who is, at the outset, not used to having a new teacher under their wing. Thus, breaking the ice with your MEO might seem a bit stressful or intimidating. So, let's explore some good ways to get to know your MEO. First, let's look at a school story.

SCHOOL STORIES

Kris Johnson

Kris is excited to be joining the learning community of Westbrook Middle School (WMS). Having recently graduated from an education program with a concentration in literature and language arts, Kris knows that WMS has one of the most reputable department chairs in the county, Mrs. Avery Dumont. Kris is thrilled to learn that Avery is going to be serving as a mentor teacher but is also very nervous about being new and fitting into the school environment.

Increasingly, Kris is worried about making a good impression on the staff, especially with Avery who is known for leading engaging professional learning workshops throughout the tri-state area. In this meeting Avery will share details about the Grade 7 and 8 students that Kris will be teaching and the scope of the full-time teaching assignment. Normally a confident and well-spoken individual, Kris is feeling rather anxious about the first in-person meeting coming up next week.

Have you ever felt the way Kris is feeling? Perhaps you are feeling this way as you get set to learn about your teaching assignment and meet your MEO for the first time? You are not alone. In chatting about our first days and weeks of our first teaching assignments (back in the day), we shared stories of how things may have seemed overwhelming at first but soon became more familiar.

Meeting someone in person for the first time, although a common experience, can evoke an array of feelings ranging from excitement to nervousness. When the person we are about to meet is our MEO or supervisor e.g. department chair, assistant principal or school principal, we sometimes struggle to find the right words to say in those initial meetings. This can seem a bit awkward or cause some anxious feelings especially when we think of all the hype around making a good first impression. These are normal feelings. The first thing to remember though, is that the person you are meeting is most likely feeling some of the same emotions you are as they get ready to meet you. This is human nature. So, to help you break the ice and find some meaningful ways to ease into getting to know the teachers and leaders who will be supporting you as a new teacher, we are going to equip you with some *meditative questions* to assist in those first few meetings.

USING MEDIATIVE QUESTIONS

What is a meditative question? A meditative question is a type of inquiry that encourages deep reflection, introspection, and self-awareness. Unlike closed-ended (yes/no) questions that seek specific information, mediative questions are open-ended and thought-provoking, prompting individuals to explore their thoughts, feelings, values, beliefs, and experiences. For example, consider this closed question: "Did you plan a movement activity in your lesson?" The answer is either yes or no. A meditative question could look like this: "How do you include movement activities in your lesson design/planning?" The style of question allows space and opportunity for deeper exploration of the topic at hand. It invites conversation and sharing ideas which is exactly what you want for that first meeting!

PUTTING THEORY INTO PRACTICE

Remember, a mediative question is one that is open-ended and leaves space for both you and the person you are speaking with to share ideas. These are not yes or no questions, rather, prompts that seek to explore ideas, attitudes, and the learning that corresponds to the topic at hand. What follows is a series of meditative questions that you can try.

Samples of Mediative Questions That You Can Use With Your Mentor Teacher	
Reflective Self-Exploration	• What were you most excited about as you embarked on your first teaching assignment? • What aspects of your teaching practice do you enjoy the most?
Understanding Goals and Expectations	• What are your short-term and long-term goals for this teaching assignment? • How do you envision success in your role as a teacher, both for yourself and for your students?
Navigating Challenges	• What are some potential challenges or concerns you anticipate encountering in this new teaching assignment? (opportunity to discuss needs of specific students). • What strategies have you used in the past to navigate difficult situations or setbacks?
Building Relationships	• How do you establish positive relationships with your students, colleagues, and parents/guardians? • What strategies do you find effective for connecting with students and creating a supportive classroom environment?
Professional Growth and Development	• How do you incorporate feedback and reflection into your ongoing professional growth? • What opportunities for professional development or learning are you interested in pursuing?
Work-Life Balance and Well-Being	• How did you maintain a healthy work-life balance in your first teaching assignment? • What self-care practices or strategies do you find helpful for managing stress and avoiding burnout?

(Continued)

(Continued)

Samples of Mediative Questions That You Can Use With Your Mentor Teacher	
Celebrating Successes	• What milestones or achievements are you looking forward to celebrating in your teaching journey this year? • How do you plan to recognize and celebrate the successes of your students and yourself?

MOVING FORWARD

Overall, mediative questions serve as powerful tools for fostering dialogue, deepening insights, and helping you to ease into new professional relationships with your MEO and other staff. What is interesting to note about these questions, is that they are questions that your MEO will most likely ask of you. These mediative questions are useful for framing other conversations and work well with students and parents.

Our hope is that these meditative questions (or others that you will create) can help both you and your MEO engage in rich dialogue, clarify goals and expectations, identify potential challenges, and cultivate strategies for success in your new teaching assignment and these first few formative years of your teaching career. In fact, prior to that first meeting, you could go for a coffee with a friend or peer and talk through some of the samples we provided. Our goal is that you will feel better equipped to have great initial discussions when meeting your MEO. Happy icebreaking! You've got this!

REFLECTIVE PRACTICE

Based upon your conversation and questions with your new colleague, reflect upon the process. How might these meditative questions help you seek out the answers to some of your questions?

BRINGING IT ALL TOGETHER

Being mindful of the presented tactics in this chapter will encourage you to meet the first days of school head on with confidence. When we sat down to brainstorm the content of this chapter, the authors wanted to impart on you that you can never be too prepared! Preparation when considered early in the school year will provide the necessary information and structures for you to thrive not only in your first days, but the whole year!

There is no doubt that the first days of teaching can insight all sorts of feelings, and emotions. It is possible for these feelings to become overwhelming and lead to a situation where you may feel unprepared. Rest assured, all of us have had similar experiences wondering if we are truly ready to take on a classroom of our own. By providing you with tangible first steps, it is our hope that you can reduce some of your anxious feelings. Some of these tactics can even be incorporated prior to the official first day (if you would like to of course). Nonetheless, the implementation tracker at the end of this chapter can help organize your thoughts during this busy time! We encourage you to reflect on the tactics we shared and try some out for yourself, use our tool on the next pages to document your efforts, successes, and even in some cases failures. Afterall, part of the learning journey is learning what not to do next time! Best wishes for success in your first days!

IMPLEMENTATION TRACKER

Attempted toolbox tactic:	
Successes:	Roadblocks:
What should I change to be more successful next time?	

Attempted toolbox tactic:	
Successes:	Roadblocks:
What should I change to be more successful next time?	

4

THE ART AND SCIENCE OF PLANNING AND LESSON DESIGN

As a new teacher, one of the most critical skills you will develop is the ability to plan effective lessons. The classroom is a dynamic environment, filled with diverse learners who each bring unique strengths, challenges, and needs. Crafting lessons that cater to these differences while ensuring that educational standards are met is both an art and a science. This chapter will guide you through the essential elements of planning and lesson design, equipping you with the tools and strategies necessary to create engaging, meaningful, and effective learning experiences for your students.

At its core, lesson planning is about envisioning the path your students will take toward achieving specific learning goals. This involves both short-range and long-range planning. Short-range planning focuses on the day-to-day activities and lessons that build toward understanding, while long-range planning involves mapping out the curriculum over an extended period, such as a semester or school year. Both are crucial for maintaining a coherent and structured approach to teaching.

Effective planning begins with understanding your objectives. What do you want your students to learn? Clear, measurable goals are the foundation of any well-designed lesson. Research has shown that specific and well-defined objectives can significantly enhance student achievement by providing clear targets for both teaching and learning (Marzano, 2017). From there, you can determine the best methods and materials to achieve these goals. High-quality resources are key to this process, and knowing how to distinguish them from lower-quality materials will significantly impact your students' learning experiences. Utilizing trusted sources, educational research, and vetted teaching aids will ensure that your lessons are both informative and engaging.

One of the challenges you may face is finding the time to plan thoroughly while managing the myriad of responsibilities that come with teaching. This is where organizational tools like planners and pacing guides become invaluable. These tools help you allocate time efficiently, ensuring that all necessary content is covered without overwhelming you or your students. Pacing guides can also assist in aligning your lessons with school-wide or district-wide standards and expectations. Research by Harris and colleagues (2010) highlights that structured planning and time management significantly improve instructional quality and student outcomes.

In today's technology-driven world, AI can be a powerful ally in lesson planning. From generating lesson ideas to creating personalized learning experiences, AI tools can save time and enhance the quality of your lessons. Such things as ClanEd's (2024) intuitive LMS system uses AI to assist teachers and students alike to personalize learning to meet the needs of a variety of students. A study by Luckin et al. (2016) suggests that AI in education can support teachers by automating routine tasks and providing data-driven insights, thereby allowing educators to focus more on instruction and student interaction. Embracing these technological advancements can provide new teachers with innovative ways to engage students and streamline the planning process.

Collaboration is another vital aspect of effective planning. Working with substitute teachers, for instance, requires clear, concise lesson plans that allow for continuity in instruction. When you need to be away from the classroom, having detailed and accessible plans ensures that learning continues smoothly in your absence. Additionally, collaborating with colleagues through professional development opportunities can provide fresh insights and new strategies for lesson design. Engaging in continuous learning and sharing best practices with peers will help you grow as an educator and keep your teaching methods current and effective. Darling-Hammond et al. (2009) found that sustained and collaborative professional development significantly enhances teaching practices and student performance.

Moreover, lesson planning is not a solitary activity but a collaborative and iterative process. Seeking feedback from mentors and peers can provide new perspectives and highlight areas for improvement. Reflective practice, where you regularly assess and refine your teaching strategies based on student outcomes and feedback, is essential for professional growth. Research by Larrivee (2008) underscores that teachers who engage in reflective practice tend to be more effective in fostering student learning. Additionally, incorporating student feedback into your planning can lead to more responsive and effective teaching, as it aligns your instruction more closely with students' needs and interests.

Ultimately, the goal of planning is to create a roadmap for learning that is flexible yet structured, challenging yet attainable. It is a process that evolves with experience and reflection. As you refine your planning skills, you will find that well-designed lessons not only enhance student learning but also make teaching more enjoyable and fulfilling.

In this chapter, we will explore various toolbox tactics and tools to help you master the art of lesson planning. From setting clear objectives and selecting quality resources to utilizing technology and engaging in professional development, you will gain a comprehensive understanding of how to design effective lessons that inspire and educate your students. By embracing these principles, you will be well on your way to becoming a confident and successful teacher, capable of making a lasting impact in the classroom.

As you embark through the rest of this chapter, we wanted to make sure you had a clear map of the concepts and ideas that will be explored more in depth. As we mentioned previously in the introduction, do not feel pressured to try and apply all of these ideas, rather explore as many of these as you can and apply what piques your interests or needs. Enjoy exploring the following toolbox tactics:

1. Short Range vs. Long Range Planning: Understanding the difference in short and long range planning will help you pace out your delivery without feeling like you need to over plan.
2. Planning for Mastery: The fundamental goal for our teaching should be student mastery of the content. By knowing how to plan for mastery we can encourage a greater potential for student growth and achievement.
3. Pacing Guides and Planners: Often the districts we serve have support mechanisms like pacing guides to help us pace our lesson delivery.

4. Subplans and Working With Substitute Teachers: Substitute or replacement teachers are an invaluable resource. Knowing more about interacting with these individuals will in turn foster long-term relationships.
5. High and Low Quality Resources: Believe it or not, there is a difference in the quality of resources. Knowing what you should and should not look for can save you time, and even money!
6. Professional Learning and Professional Development: Teachers are often presented with a caveat of PL or PD options, knowing what it out there will help you be more efficient in determining what works for you.

TOOLKIT TACTIC 4.1 SHORT RANGE VS. LONG RANGE PLANNING

Case: *Planning can and will be hard for some more than others, but it is fundamental to the success of our instruction. It can be something we all think we do very well, especially if we have the chance to practice short and long range planning in our preparation courses. Knowing where to focus our planning first will help us prioritize our time and knowing when to jump from short range to long range planning will allow us to better design units and lessons for our students.*

From Vince: *There was a time in my first few years where I would take a calendar (a few weeks before school started) and write down my daily lessons for the entire year. Guess what? By week three, my calendar was already behind and I was feeling stressed. I wish I would have known more about the importance of short-range, and long-range planning and, more importantly, the difference between them. It is okay to be prepared and know where you are headed in the long term while being more specific in the short term.*

SELF-REFLECTION (PRE-READING)

How do you currently understand short- vs. long-range planning? What might be three key differences based on your current understanding?

Planning for the delivery of content over the course of a school year can be very daunting. It can feel as though you have an insurmountable amount of content you are required to deliver, which often manifests as pages upon pages of a resource or textbook. Before blindly jumping into the deep end of content delivery, we feel it is of the utmost importance to understand the impact short-range and long-range plans can have on your instruction in the classroom.

AUTHOR'S CORNER

Vince's Experience

When my first year began, I was tasked with teaching senior-level social studies, and I really had no idea how to plan effectively. My college courses provided me with some templates I could follow, but beyond one project I did in my second or third year of school, I really didn't have an idea on what to do. So after searching online for "the best way to plan a year as a new teacher," I was met with a series of ways that I was not comfortable with. I ended up printing off my monthly calendars, looking at the resource book and dividing it into daily chunks, and proceeded to fill in the dates on the calendar with the themes of each lesson. Keep in mind I was doing this a few weeks before the school year started, and I was excited I was able to organize my life according to a calendar . . . that was, until school started.

In my calendar plan, I did not account for unplanned interruptions such as the pace at which my students learn, or school field trips. So essentially after only two weeks, my calendar year plan (which I had spent hours on) was not helpful whatsoever. I was so disappointed that in my haste to plan out my year, I only focused on "getting through the course" rather than considering the best way to teach the course to my students.

If you read my experience and thought to yourself "Me too, Vince," then I appreciate that I am not the only one who was stressed out with the idea of planning a course (or more) that I had never previously taught. It is a challenging task on its own, but balancing this with all the other pressures new teachers feel can feel insurmountable. That is why we feel it is imperative to consider the following differences when we are short range and long range plans.

CONSIDERATIONS FOR SHORT VS. LONG RANGE PLANNING

OBJECTIVES AND STANDARDS ALIGNMENT

- *Short-Range Planning:* Focuses on daily or weekly lessons, ensuring each lesson has clear, measurable objectives that align with the curriculum standards.
- *Long-Range Planning*: Involves mapping out the curriculum for a semester or school year, ensuring that all standards and objectives will be covered over time. It provides a big-picture view to ensure cumulative learning.

SCOPE AND SEQUENCE

- *Short-Range Planning*: Addresses immediate learning goals and activities. It's essential to sequence lessons logically to build on prior knowledge and scaffold new concepts.
- *Long-Range Planning:* Involves creating a roadmap that sequences units and major topics throughout the year. It ensures that foundational skills are taught first, followed by more complex concepts.

FLEXIBILITY AND ADAPTABILITY

- *Short-Range Planning:* Needs to be flexible to respond to daily classroom dynamics, student understanding, and unforeseen events. Adjustments can be made more readily.
- *Long-Range Planning*: Provides a structured plan but should include flexibility for adjustments based on student progress, feedback, and unexpected interruptions (e.g., snow days, school events).

ASSESSMENT AND EVALUATION

- *Short-Range Planning:* Includes formative assessments to monitor student understanding and guide immediate instructional decisions.
- *Long-Range Planning:* Incorporates summative assessments to evaluate overall student progress and mastery of content over extended periods. It helps in planning major assessments and projects.

RESOURCE ALLOCATION

- *Short-Range Planning:* Involves selecting and preparing daily instructional materials and resources. It requires finding high-quality resources that align with the specific day's lesson.
- *Long-Range Planning:* Involves gathering and organizing resources for entire units or semesters. It includes planning for the acquisition of books, technology, and other materials in advance.

TIME MANAGEMENT

- *Short-Range Planning:* Requires daily or weekly time management to ensure each lesson fits within the allotted time and progresses efficiently.
- *Long-Range Planning*: Involves macro-level or unit time management to ensure that the entire curriculum can be covered within the school year, with adequate time for review and enrichment.

REFLECTION AND ITERATION

- *Short-Range Planning:* Involves daily or weekly reflection on what worked well and what didn't, allowing for quick iteration and improvement.
- *Long-Range Planning:* Involves periodic reflection on the effectiveness of units and the overall curriculum plan, with adjustments made for future planning cycles.

SELF-REFLECTION (POST-READING)

How might you organize your planning schedule to address the key differences between short-range and long-range plans?

Which of the attributes above would you feel you have the most confidence with? Which may require more practice or attention?

Having clarity of what should be considered when looking at short-range and long-range planning will help to organize our thoughts around what should be addressed next in our classrooms. While this list is not exhaustive by any means, it is intended to provide an understanding of some of the main considerations, as well as the intended foci for the considerations both in the short and long term. To be blunt, balancing short-term and long-term planning can be confusing especially if you are teaching a subject area that you aren't so familiar with. Our suggestion for this would be to talk to a mentor or a colleague who may have experience in this area. Here are a few suggestion talking points you may want to use to help your conversation.

TALKING TO A COLLEAGUE ABOUT PLANNING

1. How rigid are you with your long range plans? To what extent do these operate as more of a guide and less of a rigid plan?
2. How do you prepare for expected and unexpected interruptions to your schedule? Do you leave some spare days, or gaps in the planning calendar?
3. How do you know what is necessary to include vs. nice to include?

REFLECTIVE PRACTICE

Reread through the list of considerations above, and make a commitment to improve your understanding of one that is currently unclear to you. Often your school or district may have some resources available to you to assist in clarifying your understanding. Don't forget that you can also ask questions! No question is too straightforward, especially in your first few years. We guarantee someone else has or has had the same questions you do about planning!

TOOLKIT TACTIC 4.2 PLANNING FOR MASTERY

Case: *We all want every one of our students to experience mastery of their learning as they learn from us. Mastery of students learning only happens when we plan to do so by design, rather than leave it up to chance. This means, we truly must know what mastery means to both our students and ourselves and then from there take actionable steps to include these considerations in our planning process.*

From Tim: *As a new teacher, it was tempting for me to rush through the curriculum to keep up with time constraints. In essence, I was teaching* *at my pace, not the pace of my learners. I soon noticed gaps in some of my students' learning. The deep comprehension and skill-building inherent to mastery learning is crucial for our students' long-term success as they are not left behind, but rather supported to achieve success at their own pace. For new teachers, implementing mastery learning encourages a more thoughtful and individualized approach to teaching, fostering an environment where every student can thrive.*

MASTERY OF LEARNING

Ensuring students achieve mastery in their learning is a key goal for teachers. With the potential to considerably accelerate student learning (according to the *Visible Learning* research, Hattie, 2023), mastery learning refers to an instructional approach where students are given the time and resources necessary to learn specific knowledge and skills prior to moving onto the next topic. Essentially it means students can really understand the material before moving on, and this requires thoughtful planning and execution that balances the following considerations: pacing and planning using progressions, clear learning objectives, formative and summative assessments, and vertical and horizontal considerations. Establishing a classroom that plans for mastery is easier said than done, and often takes time and experience. In no way are there expectations that this can be created immediately, however we feel it is important to lay the foundation for mastery instruction by ensuring we plan for it. Here are some strategies for you to consider as students move toward mastery in your classroom.

PACING AND PLANNING USING PROGRESSIONS

Creating learning progressions means mapping out the steps students need to take to move from their current level of understanding to mastering the standards or objectives. This process involves breaking down standards into smaller, manageable learning targets. One way to think about it is if the standard or curricular objective is the whole meal, how might we break this down into logical bite-size chunks for our learners?

We suggest starting by unpacking the standards to identify the key skills and concepts students need to master. Then, develop a sequence of learning progression statements that build on each other. Each statement should align with the overall objective and be designed to deepen students' understanding progressively. Heritage and Popham

(2020) note that well-designed learning progressions provide a roadmap for instruction and assessment, ensuring that each step in the learning process is purposeful and connected. We have included both a template and an example for you to explore (Figures 4.1 and 4.2).

A Template to Create Progressions

Standard or Curricular Objective: *Copy and paste the specific standard into this box.*	
Concepts (Nouns): *List all of the concepts that are located within the standard here.*	Skills (Verbs): *List all of the skills located in the standard here.*
Learning Progressions: *Create a logical progression of statements here that students will be required to know as they build toward mastery within their learning.*	

Source: Fisher, D., Frey, N., Almarode, J. T., Barbee, K., Amador, O., & Assof, J. (2024). *The Teacher Clarity Playbook, Grades K-12: A Hands-On Guide to Creating Learning Intentions and Success Criteria for Organized, Effective Instruction* (2nd ed). Corwin.

A Sample of Learning Progressions

Standard or Curricular Objective: CCSS.ELA-LITERACY.W.2.3 (California 2nd Grade ELA - Writing) Write narratives in which students recount a well-elaborated event or short sequence of events, include details to describe actions, thoughts, and feelings, use temporal words to signal event order, and provide a sense of closure.	
Concepts (Nouns): • narratives • event (sequence of events) • actions • thoughts • feelings • temporal words • sense of closure	Skills (Verbs): • write • recount • describe actions • signal event order
Learning Progressions: 1. Students can introduce their story by recounting events (talking, and describing). 2. Students can identify the appropriate sequence of events by using terms like *first, next, last*. 3. Students can expand on their story by using action words, and describing feelings (in voice). 4. Students can put their story into writing, using a graphic organizer for support. 5. Students can include an introduction, supporting details, and a conclusion in writing.	

Source: California Department of Education, https://www2.cde.ca.gov/cacs/id/web/5627

When breaking up standards (or curricular objectives) into progressions, it can be challenging to consider what logical order works best. One thing we would like to remind you is that what is more important is the actual creation of these progressions, the order may not matter as much. Naturally that does depend on which standard you are addressing, and other vertical and horizontal contexts (which will be discussed in a few paragraphs). One thing that helped me (Vince) was looking at verbs that are allocated to specific levels of Bloom's Taxonomy (or Depth of Knowledge if that's what your school/district uses). By using this tool as a map we can connect surface level skills to deeper levels of skills in our progressions, and the progressions become more strategically aligned with the mastery approach. We have provided a sample of this document in the appendix, and we recommend you use the verbs within the document to help you create the necessary progressions of learning.

FORMATIVE ASSESSMENTS TO TRACK MASTERY

Formative assessments should be embedded within these progressions to monitor student progress and inform instruction. Teachers should use assessment data to identify where students are struggling and adjust their teaching strategies accordingly. Fuchs et al. (2019) stress the importance of data-driven decision-making in enhancing student achievement by ensuring instruction meets students' needs. We will spend more time in Chapter 7 discussing the importance of assessments in our classrooms, however we felt it was important to highlight formative assessments than their role in planning for mastery here as well. Frequent formative assessments are crucial to track student progress toward mastery. These can include quizzes, exit tickets, and think-pair-share activities. Black and Wiliam (2018) emphasize that formative assessments help identify gaps in knowledge so teachers can intervene quickly. Using information from these assessments in our grade-level meetings, staff meetings, and instructional reflections will help us be more deliberate in constructing a classroom that is designed for student mastery.

HORIZONTAL VS. VERTICAL PLANNING CONSIDERATIONS

Considering horizontal and vertical planning will help us better understand the impact that our colleagues also have on students outside the walls of our classroom. It can be overwhelming to look at all of the standards or objectives we are expected to teach our students, and we have found that the best solution to this can be a conversation with your colleagues in your grade level as well as others in your school. We call this horizontal and vertical planning. Horizontal planning involves teachers at the same grade level or subject area working together. This ensures that students receive a consistent learning experience across different classes. For example, all third-grade teachers might coordinate to teach the same science unit at the same time, sharing resources and strategies to ensure all students have a similar learning experience. It is also possible we may glean some great ideas from our colleagues, thus improving the collective efficacy of our grade-level teachers. One consideration for horizontal planning (sometimes referred to as PLC [Professional Learning Community] time) is that conversations about instruction and student learning should ALWAYS have data to support your decisions. We often say, a conversation about students without data is just an opinion!

Although we may be responsible for teaching students in a particular grade, it is also imperative that we are aware of the skills required in the previous grade and the next grade. Not only does this help us diagnose what prior knowledge is required of our students when they come into our classroom, it also helps us understand what they need to master prior to their next grade. This is where vertical planning can be an asset to us. Vertical planning involves coordinating the curriculum and instruction across different grade levels. This ensures a smooth progression of skills and knowledge as students move through their education. Vertical planning helps avoid gaps and redundancies in the curriculum and makes sure students build on their prior knowledge as they advance. DuFour and Fullan (2013) highlight that effective vertical planning fosters a more coherent learning journey for students. This also can offer some reprieve when we find the skills required in some of our standards tend to repeat year after year, and may help to answer the question "How far back do I need to set the foundation for my students' new learning?"

Both horizontal and vertical planning are essential for mastery learning. Horizontal planning ensures consistency and equity, while vertical planning ensures continuity and progression. Engaging in both planning practices helps us to create a comprehensive classroom experience that supports mastery. Ensuring students move toward mastery requires careful planning, both horizontally and vertically, and creating coherent learning progressions from standards or objectives. By setting clear objectives, using formative assessments, providing timely feedback, and differentiating instruction, teachers can create a learning environment where all students have the opportunity to achieve high levels of understanding and success.

REFLECTIVE PRACTICE

As you think about planning for mastery, consider your strengths and interests as a learner. This would be a great place to start unpacking standards or objectives. It can be quite overwhelming to teach a topic, or grade level that is new or unfamiliar to you and we want you to know that it's okay and a natural feeling. It is imperative that you use the collective experience of those around you to help guide your planning process. Planning in isolation can be frustrating and discouraging. Remember, we have all been there and we all have experiences that we can lend to help the planning process go more smoothly.

QUESTIONS TO ASK YOUR MENTOR OR COLLEAGUES

1. Does our school use common language in our planning, instruction, and assessments to provide consistency among all teachers?
2. How might you organize this specific standard to move from surface to transfer mastery for your students?
3. Does our district have samples of learning progression documents, horizontal planning documents, or vertical planning documents I should be aware of?

TOOLKIT TACTIC 4.3 PACING GUIDES AND PLANNERS

Case: *Intended to support teachers as they engage in the process of balancing content delivery with timing, there are different iterations of pacing guides and planners. It is important to understand that not all guides are created equally, thus we should maintain a critical approach when looking at the different types of guides and planners.*

From Sarah: *The best way to stay on top of your workload is to make note of it. This is not a PSA to buy an $80.00 planner and fancy pens; of course, if you choose to, that's great! For some, using a planner is unproductive. For others, the act of crossing things off to-do lists or tossing out completed sticky notes is a better solution. Do what's best for you! This may change overtime; it did for me and I find now that the rhythm I have is something that keeps me on track with all of my responsibilities. When it comes to guides, connect with likeminded or grade partners for a plan. My first-grade partner (Hi Nicole!) and I worked out a system where we combined both of our Grade 3 classrooms for guided reading every morning. This was after learning about and getting to know our students, looking at our curricular outcomes and pacing guides, filling in our incredible educational assistant (Hi Anita!), and going over feedback at the end of the day together. Work with the people around you to tackle the outcomes connected to a pacing or a learning guide. Some of my best learning in my first couple of years came from the people right next door.*

Stepping into the classroom, navigating all the new that comes with your first few days, weeks, or months can naturally be overwhelming, especially when it comes to planning. We can remember asking ourselves, "Where do I begin?" when it comes to a place to start the year. Is it page 1 in my provided resource? (Perhaps). Is it the first standard or outcome in my mandated content? (Also perhaps). Rather than wonder and randomly select based on your own understanding, or based upon what you learned in your credentialing program we suggest figuring out if your school district or school itself has a pacing guide, or a guided planner document that is intended to support the delivery or your program. These can also be known as roadmaps, or planners, or even in some cases a curriculum delivery schedule and depending on your district, they may be enforced at greater degrees than others. Our recommendation is to inquire about these resources, as on many occasions these have outlined priorities and can serve as a more specific support than something you may find online or other places.

PACING GUIDES VS. RESOURCE PROVIDED TOOLS

PACING GUIDES

Pacing guides are documents that outline the schedule for teaching particular units, topics, or standards within a curriculum. They provide a timeline for when specific content should be taught, ensuring that the curriculum is completed within the allotted time. Pacing guides help maintain consistency across different classes and schools, particularly important in districts aiming for uniformity in educational outcomes. In many districts, these guides are created by district consultants or representatives that can also provide professional learning to support the delivery of the content. In our experience, there is a general misunderstanding surrounding the intention and purpose of these types of documents. Often it is assumed that these are created to force teachers to teach in a certain way. This cannot be further from the intended purpose. In general, these documents are intended to provide a roadmap of essential knowledge, skills, and dispositions we are required to teach our students. We cannot speak for all districts and schools who incorporate these guides, but our recommendation should be that these are used to guide teachers rather than force them into required teaching practices. While the look and design of each guide can be different, most have the following components:

1. *Timeline:* Breaks down the academic year into weeks or months, specifying what should be taught during each period. This helps in avoiding content overload toward the end of the term and ensures a steady flow of information.
2. *Standards and Objectives:* Lists the learning goals and standards to be addressed in each unit or lesson. These are often aligned with state or national standards, ensuring that all necessary skills and knowledge areas are covered.
3. *Resources and Materials:* Suggests textbooks, digital resources, and other materials needed for teaching the content. This could include specific chapters, articles, multimedia resources, and supplementary tools.
4. *Assessments:* Indicates when formative (ongoing) and summative (end-of-unit) assessments should be administered to gauge student understanding. This could include quizzes, exams, projects, and presentations.

5. *Key Activities and Projects:* Highlights important activities, projects, or labs that support the learning objectives. These activities are designed to engage students and enhance their understanding of the material.

Benefits

- *Structured Progression:* Ensures that teachers cover all necessary material without rushing or lingering too long on a single topic. It allows for a logical sequence of content delivery.
- *Alignment with Standards:* Helps align instruction with state or national educational standards, ensuring that students are prepared for standardized tests and assessments.
- *Flexibility:* Provides a framework that teachers can adapt to meet the needs of their students. Teachers can adjust the pacing based on the progress and understanding of their students.

RESOURCE PROVIDED TOOLS

Resource provided or resource recommended pacing guides are also prevalent in our schools and classrooms. These guides are generally intended to support the delivery and teaching of the resource over the course of the school year. While most resources are created with the intention exclusively using the content to address the subject matter in its entirety, it is generally accepted that within your classroom these resources should be used to *support your instruction* rather than *drive your instruction*. Thus if you are teaching multiple subjects or content areas, there is a good chance you will have multiple resources. Later in this chapter, we address the differences between high value resources and low value resources, so for now we will just be focusing on the instructional guides that are supplied with your resources.

It is imperative to understand that these resources are generally created by a group of people who have the greatest intention of addressing all the required standards. The catch is the textbook or online resource you are using is written from their perspectives and may require a critical approach as you seek to pace your instruction around these resources. In the box that follows you will find some questions or considerations that should be made as you seek to blend the pacing of resources with the pacing of your instruction. If you are unable to answer these questions on your own, we recommend finding a colleague who may be able to provide more clarity as you engage in your resource driven planning.

REFLECTION QUESTIONS AND CONSIDERATIONS FOR USING RESOURCE PACING GUIDES

1. Is this the only resource I will be using to support my instruction, or are there multiple resources intended to support me?
2. What documents does my district or school have to help support my instruction that may counter the messaging in the resource pacing guide?
3. To what extent does this resource address the required standards or learning objectives I am obliged to teach? (Remember, just because a standard or objective is listed in the resource, does not mean the resource addresses the entirety).
4. How do my colleagues or grade-level partners use the pacing guides and teacher resource to support their instruction?
5. To what extent does this pacing guide reflect the desires and intentions of my grade-level planning processes (It is possible that your colleagues teach the course in a different order than presented in the resource, and that is okay!)
6. Does the pacing of this resource reflect the perspectives, and attitudes of myself as a professional, my school, or my students? (Some resources are more centrally focused in the information they present, and it is possible they may not reflect the uniqueness of your local context).
7. Are there support documents from colleagues or friends outside of your school district that may better support your instructional practices?

THE INTEGRATION OF PACING GUIDES AND LESSON PLANNING

When used together, pacing guides and lesson planning can provide a comprehensive approach to curriculum delivery. Pacing guides offer the big-picture view, helping teachers map out the entire course and can serve as a long-term plan ensuring coverage of all required standards. Lesson planning naturally provide the day-to-day details, ensuring that each lesson contributes to the overall goals outlined in the pacing guide. They help in breaking down the larger goals into manageable daily tasks. More often than not, the use of pacing guides to support lesson planning will make your instruction more focused, and intentional. Please read the excerpt below from Stephen, a new teacher who was tasked with teaching a combined-grade classroom. His school used a version of pacing guides they called roadmaps to ensure there was consistency in delivery of content, as well as more deliberate collaborative planning periods with grade-level colleagues.

VOICES FROM THE FIELD

Stephen Ellis

El Dorado Elementary School

Teaching is always something I wanted to pursue as a career. I accepted a position at my site to teach a combined class of first- and second-grade students. I faced significant challenges in my first year when I finally stepped into that role. The job caught me off guard and monopolized my time and mental energy. I started the year feeling overwhelmed and very unsure of myself. However, I stepped in to work with a team that had spent the previous school year writing their roadmap. This roadmap covers the standards determined by our state for teaching ELA and mathematics throughout the school year. I still brought too much work home and gave up a lot of myself to improve as much as I could during the school year as fast as possible. Even still, I still had the luxury of watching fantastic teachers who had created this living document to plan our school year's work.

The support system we developed was more than just a guidebook—it was a testament to the power of collaboration and community in education. As a team, we transformed it into a comprehensive repository of resources, creating a spreadsheet filled with links to various documents that we needed throughout the year. This made our collaborative lesson planning for the upcoming week much more manageable. Whenever we felt uncertain about the direction of our instruction, we relied on this roadmap. It provided easy access to pre- and postassessments, which was incredibly helpful when starting or finishing a new unit. Working with a group of experienced teachers and using this shared document not only enriched my first year of teaching but also made it much more productive than I could have ever imagined.

In summary, pacing guides can be a vital tool for effective teaching, ensuring that educational goals are met in a structured and organized manner. They can help you manage your time, resources, and instructional strategies to maximize student learning, promoting consistency and quality across classrooms. Having a document with common and shared language across a school and district also reduces the potential variance between classrooms, which promotes a collaborative environment where all teachers (regardless of tenure or years of experience) can be a part of the conversation that focuses on student learning, growth, and progress.

TOOLBOX TACTIC 4.4 SUB PLANS AND WORKING WITH SUBSTITUTE TEACHERS

> ***Case:*** *Catching a cold, feeling run down, needing a mental health break from the classroom are all exceptionally valid reasons for taking a day to rest and recuperate. Often new teachers are reluctant to take a day for themselves because making plans for a substitute is often more work than coming in sick. This is easily offset with some mild preparation and having access to trusted substitute teachers.*
>
> ***From Vince:*** *Do you have a sub or supply teacher you can call, and rely on? This subtle but significant resource can be the difference between having to miss a day with your students and be worried the whole time or taking time for yourself knowing that you have a replacement teacher you can trust. Having contingency plans and contacts will be the insurance you need to ensure your time off is taken for yourself when needed.*

SUBSTITUTE TEACHERS

The inevitable will happen—you're going to get sick, have an appointment, experience a loss, or simply will need to take a personal day for some much needed rest and self-care. Life happens! In your first few years of teaching, it may seem easier to go into work sick, grieving, or burnt out; however, that is unnecessary. You can't possibly be a great teacher for your students if you don't take care of yourself first and foremost. Truth be told, that is sometimes easier said than done.

Emergency substitute plans to the rescue! Substitute teachers (also known as replacement teachers or guest teachers) are a vital part of the profession. Substitute teaching is one of the most thankless jobs in education, and yet, we need substitute teachers in our field to provide support when called upon. It's important to remember a few things when planning to have a substitute teacher take over for you in your classroom, whether it be for a day, a week, or much longer.

INTRODUCE YOURSELF

It is so important to introduce yourself to your substitute, even though you may never meet in person. Express gratitude for their ability to replace you for the time you'll be away. Allow them the opportunity to leave their contact information and notes on each subject covered. I have found that leaving a coffee pod, a treat, or some candy was a great way to show my gratitude. Another thing that sometimes is overlooked is letting them know things about the school that they may not know, for example, where the staff bathrooms are, where they may find a microwave at lunch, or a place they can go during a prep or at recess. All of these things are important so that the substitute feels like a part of your school community and welcome to be there.

SUBSTITUTE CONTINUITY

When I (Sarah) was in the classroom, I was lucky enough to find a brilliant substitute teacher who became my main contact when I was away. He knew what my rules were, what I was flexible on, and how I liked my classroom to be kept. I was so thankful that, whenever I needed him for eight years, Mr. O'Scolai could fill in for me. It also helped my students when I was away because he was a familiar face. When I knew I would be away, I would tell my students and the first question I would get is, "Is it Mr. O?" They enjoyed his teaching style, his examples, and his humor, so I knew that my students were in great hands whenever I called him. If you have the ability to do the same, it is highly recommended.

KEEP EVERYTHING CURRENT AND UP TO DATE

Your class roster, emergency binder (in case of a fire drill, lockdown, or other emergency), supervision schedule, class schedule, and student guide should be frequently kept current. It is important for a substitute teacher to know which students you have in your classroom. If you have students that have moved away, update your list. If you have students that require assistance or pull-out support, make that known. If you have a student who could be of great assistance to the substitute teacher, note it! Things like this will ensure things are kept status quo for the students, and, nine times out of ten, will keep the classroom running smoothly when you're away. An emergency binder or folder is typically provided by your employer. It will have muster points, instructions to follow during a lockdown or fire drill, and emergency numbers. Always include this for the substitute teacher in your room to review before the day begins. It's also important for the substitute teacher to know of your supervision schedule, should you have supervision at recess, lunch, before, or after school. This is to continue monitored safety for all children, and so it is vital that this is communicated to the substitute.

REVIEW CLASSROOM PROCEDURES WITH STUDENTS OFTEN

At the beginning of the year, take the opportunity to coconstruct rules, nonnegotiables, and procedures with your class. It's a wonderful way to give voice and choice to students. It also provides you with an accountability pillar when you need to review these procedures and rules with your students. Take the opportunity, monthly, to review these procedures and rules with your class, so that, even when there is a guest in the room, things run smoothly for everyone.

HIGH TECHNOLOGY

Prebook any technology that your substitute may need to use with your class. Consider leaving QR codes for your substitute that lead to videos, articles, or games that they can use with your class. I got into the habit of filming more difficult concepts and sending them to my substitute so that they could see how I wanted a topic or strand taught. It also helped my students to see those videos. Sometimes, I would film myself reading the next chapter of our novel study and leave that for my substitute to play, and let him use prompts for discussion or activities. However you choose to leverage technology, make it seamless. Don't leave things that require your personal log-in information or passwords. Always use your school district credentials to share QR codes and videos. Most importantly, keep a copy of your student's passwords and usernames for whatever technology and websites they will be using that day.

LOW TECHNOLOGY

Not every school has one-to-one device access, robotics, labs, or classroom carts full of tech options. That is okay. If you have the ability, include a photocopy or template with your plans so that your substitute can easily have copies made by a grade partner, educational assistant, or administrative assistant. Better yet, leave a class set for your substitute! If you have access to a document camera, your substitute can utilize that, as well, to save on paper, if you happen to be at a school where copies are limited or your school has a go-green initiative.

CURRICULUM STRANDS AND EARLY FINISHERS

The body of your plans should include curriculum connections, as well as past connections for students. Leave teacher guides readily available for your substitute to see where these things fit in the grand scheme. Allow lots of time for students to work and practice during this time. Sometimes, less is more. Some students may complete tasks early. Have something for early finishers to work on that isn't just free time on a device. Perhaps they are helping their peers, working on an ongoing project, silently reading, or doing some enrichment. Many teachers have an early finishers binder or handout; this can be helpful, especially if students are used to seeing or using this.

No substitute plans will be perfect. Your plans may be followed to a tee sometimes, while in other situations, your substitute teacher may need to improvise and work on the fly. Either way, substitute teachers are an asset to our school districts and should be treated as professional colleagues, not babysitters. They are trained professionals who want the opportunity to use what they went to school for. Don't be afraid to leave detailed plans with lots of things to cover; it's better to have too much rather than not enough. Leaving a movie can be okay in some instances, but shouldn't be the go-to for replacement teachers in your room. Your students will be in great hands while you're away!

SELF-REFLECTION (POST-READING)

- Do you currently have a substitute or emergency binder? If so, is it updated with the appropriate information?
- What might you add to your current binder? What might you reconsider?
- What are some of your best practices when it comes to making substitute teachers feel welcome in your classroom or school?

TOOLKIT TACTIC 4.5 HIGH- AND LOW-QUALITY RESOURCES

> ***Case:*** *It is your first year and you are teaching some courses that you are very unfamiliar with, what do you do? You could ask your grade-level partner for access to their cloud folder that has thousands of files on it, you could ask AI for help, you could look at your textbooks and other resources, you could scour online for paid resources . . . The options are endless, however the options are not all good. It is important to know the difference between high and low quality resources and how they should be used in the classroom.*
>
> ***From Wayne:*** *Very early in my career, I was struggling to keep up with my lesson prep, coaching, editing the yearbook and a host of other activities that teachers take on. When I would look at the content standards and try to build lessons, I would quickly find myself going down rabbit holes, compiling copious amounts of resources. Quickly I decided that I would not use more than a few reliable resources and one or two extra pieces to illustrate a point I was trying to make. This helped me (and the students) avoid being buried under an avalanche of resources.*

What we present to students is just as important as the method we use to present, when it comes to curricular outcomes. In an ever-changing landscape of education, some teachers lean on workbooks, Blackline Masters, and handouts, while others are strictly using Google Classroom and nothing else. There are teachers who use STEM and robotics to teach all curricular subject areas and others who use play-based learning techniques to support their learning objectives. If you're anything like me (Sarah), you use a combination of all of these approaches in your classroom each day.

There are many websites and subscription companies that offer and sell resources for teachers to use in their classrooms (which we discuss below). Rather than spend your own money on these resources, it's important to take inventory of a few things:

1. **What learning goals and standards are you hoping to cover with the resource?**

   It's important to consider the program of studies or standards in your province, state, or territory. Ask yourself these questions: Specifically, what am I trying to cover? How will this outside resource achieve this learning goal? To what extent does this resource address the standards or outcomes I am required to teach?

2. **What already exists, courtesy of your school district or other school districts?**

   Many school districts have dedicated web pages or resource hubs that offer resources created by curricular, wellness, and equity consultants. These folks are tasked with finding and creating resources true to their subject area of expertise. Consultants will break down learning goals with multiple modes of representation in mind, multiple types of learners, and will often consider high-tech delivery versus low-tech delivery. They are tasked with keeping many things at the forefront to ensure equitable delivery for all students.

3. **What is the cost of the resource?**

   Often, to purchase a resource for use at school, someone at your school with a school purchase card will ask to know what the purchase is and why it is necessary for the learning goal you hope to achieve. Schools are accountable for every penny spent and need to be able to speak on the purchases they make. If you wish to buy a resource with your own money, so be it; however, you will be asked on how it ties to the learning goals that exist for your grade and subject level. It's important to check what already exists so that you don't have to spend your own money on resources that may already exist, but just take some time to find.

4. **What sources are cited in the making of this resource?**

   Content creators and those making resources as a secondary source of income aren't obligated to cite their sources. In trusting resources without citation as classroom material, we enter dangerous territory. If there happen to be particular biases that shine through, wrong dates, misspelled names or places, or even points that aren't rooted in fact, we run the risk of presenting incorrect information to students. School boards will often lean on certain textbooks or workbooks for classroom learning, as well as particular websites or YouTube channels to help with teaching concepts. While those may not be 100 percent perfect, they have been vetted and sourced by teams of people within a school board to ensure that what is being presented to students is appropriate and factual.

5. **Is the information presented accurate and current?**

   Part of your professional obligation as a teacher is to ensure that what you present to students as a learning tool has accurate information. Language evolves often, and it is paramount that the terms used in the resources presented reflect that. Additionally, we should strive to keep up to date in the manner in which content is presented to students. Students learn in a variety of ways, and so we must keep up with this so as to support all of the different types of learners in front of us. Being able to see a page of citations or references helps to solidify that need.

6. **Could you leverage community leaders and elders to support the learning goals you hope to cover?**

   An incredible way to continue learning ourselves is to seek out community members and cultural elders to be guest presenters or facilitators for activities and lessons in the classroom. More often than not, a student's grandmother would be more than happy to come in to talk about what it was like to move to this country from their homeland, or a kokum (Cree for *grandmother*) may be willing to come in to provide a lesson on making certain Indigenous delicacies. It is a great way to continue to strengthen home and school relationships beyond a phone call with bad news or a signature in an agenda. The life lessons that can be provided by those in our very community are worth their weight in gold and will do much more for students than a worksheet found on the internet will.

CONSIDERATIONS FOR ONLINE RESOURCES

To put it bluntly, paying money for a resource online does not necessarily make it more valuable and often you will be able to find or create a better resource yourself. Now this may come across as a hot take, but bear with us. We understand the realities of being a teacher, sometimes we do not have enough time or energy to create something new so we purchase a resource online. We have all done it, and that is okay! The way I (Vince) view these websites is sort of like a drive-thru restaurant . . . they serve a purpose when we are in a pinch and need some sustenance. However, having a drive-thru meal three times a day, 365 days a year is most likely not sustainable. Paid online resources are a platform we should explore for certain things, but we should not be spending all our time and money shopping for handouts and worksheets! We recommend that you explore places closer to you for resources, as they may be better suited to the local context of your classroom.

THE USAGE OF RESOURCES

One of the challenges when using resources that are not homegrown by colleagues or created by us for classroom use is the degree to which these resources are applicable students? If you cannot come up with a concrete answer, then we should determine what the purpose of these resources might be. Marcia Tate (author of Worksheets Don't Grow Dendrites, 2010; Engaging the Brain, 2024; and other brain-based learning books) supports this claim by asking this question: What can you do when students would rather socialize than pay attention to your lesson? It is okay for us to maintain a critical eye when considering the implementation of specific resources, after all the point of our critical eye is to have a greater impact on our students. The ultimate goal of resources is to support your instruction as a teacher, and not replace you as a teacher so please keep this in mind as you expand your search for resources as support!

SELF-REFLECTION (POST-READING)

- Have you considered looking at neighboring school district websites to find what you may be looking for?
- How often do you connect with other teachers in your building? Is there someone in the same grade group that you could ask about certain learning goals?

QUESTIONS TO ASK YOUR MENTOR OR COLLEAGUES

1. Where might I find resources to help my classroom instruction that are also supported by our school or district?
2. What is our grade-level, or department policy on sharing resources?
3. Are there recommended resources you use that you have found helpful to your instruction?

TOOLKIT TACTIC 4.6 PROFESSIONAL LEARNING AND PROFESSIONAL DEVELOPMENT

Case: *Schools have PD days, districts have PD sessions, and you are expected to continue with your own professional learning (PL). With so many sessions, it can be difficult to know where to start. Understanding the different types of workshop offerings will help you make sense of what you should or should not attend, and will also provide some reasons as to why attending sessions with your friends may not always be the best idea!*

From Wayne: *I remember my first district professional development day. I cannot remember any of the sessions or what the keynote said as it was all one-and-done type sessions. However, I can remember clearly an ongoing group led by Elders from the first community I taught in, who worked in the school and invited me and others to sit and learn with them over my first few years in teaching and the lasting impact that had on me as a teacher and a person. Not all learning opportunities are created equally—pick wisely!*

Teachers are lifelong learners. You may have heard this statement before and although some may disagree, we believe that teaching is a craft that we continuously develop and hone after time. While that may be discouraging to hear as a newer teacher that doesn't mean you can't engage in developing your skills early in your career. Many teachers continue their education by continuing onto graduate degrees like a masters or doctorate degree, yet that is not the only way to grow your capacity. There are also plenty of professional development (PD) or professional learning (PL) opportunities for teachers, and yet the common concern is determining what to attend. We thought it would be valuable to explore the various types of PD or PL available so that you can make a more informed decision.

First thing is first though, what is the difference between professional development and professional learning? Although some school districts may use these terms to describe the same thing, it is important to know their true meaning. Please make sure you clarify with your mentor what the specific local vernacular is, as you consider what we mean by PD and PL.

Professional Development	Professional Learning
• A more formal event with an established agenda created without the input of teachers • Generally a one-and-done type of event (e.g., keynote speaker, education conference, guest presenter at the school) • Emphasizes the sharing of important information, skills, and/or strategies • Little to no pressure on attendees to implement strategies; little accountability of results • Rooted in research	• Can be one event, but is more likely a series of events intended to support teachers in the classroom, school improvement, or district improvement • Can be kicked off with a speaking event, but usually the consultant or leader will engage in multiple follow up sessions to further the learning • Emphasis on development of skills, implementing new ideas, knowledge or strategies • Attendees act as partners who try new ideas and strategies. Accountability for teachers to try in a nonevaluative manner • Rooted in research

Professional development sessions and professional learning workshops also generally have different types, layouts, or agendas. We thought it would be helpful to identify the types of PD and PL as well. Please keep in mind this may not always be the case, but in general here is how you can identify whether your session is more focused PD or PL.

TYPES OF PROFESSIONAL DEVELOPMENT

- *Large Yearly Conferences:* These conferences are usually held once a year, and they have a series of keynote speakers as well as breakout sessions intended to support new learning. These types of conferences are great for connecting with likeminded individuals, and for learning on a large scale. These are not great for personalized learning experiences.
- *District Supported PD Days*: Often school districts will host a few days out of the school year that intend to mimic the larger yearly conferences in structure (keynote, and breakout sessions). Often these days are mandatory and the content may be restricted to district focused priorities. These days are great for learning more about the initiatives of your school district. If there are choices available, we recommend checking in with a colleague or mentor regarding which to attend!

- *Local Learning Consortia PD Days*: Often regions are supported by an education service district or similar area organizations that provide collaborative, high-quality, equitable, and locally responsive professional development services. Services often include face-to-face sessions, such as workshops, presentations and qualification programs; online learning opportunities, such as webinars and webcasts of face-to-face sessions; job-embedded personalized professional learning, such as collaborative planning, support to professional learning communities, and elbow-to-elbow work with individuals; and asynchronous learning and professional development resources.

TYPES OF PROFESSIONAL LEARNING

- *Consultant and School Partnerships:* On occasion, schools and districts will partner with external consultants or external experts to assist with the implementation of initiatives. These partnerships often involve multiday workshops intended to support teachers as they shift their practice and try out new learning. These partnerships are great for teachers to glean new information, try it out, and get feedback on their impact.
- *District Supported Implementation:* When districts engage in the implementation of new initiatives (curricular change, implementation of new pedagogy, new teaching strategies), they often will support teachers internally through an instructional coach framework. Sometimes called *internal consultants*, or teachers on assignment, these individuals are there to support your needs in the classroom. As a new teacher, use these resources that are available to you because oftentimes these people have been privy to this information for a while and they also understand how to make things work in your local context.
- *Voluntary Mentorship Programs*: As a new teacher some of the best professional learning we can have is not content, or pedagogy related but rather one that focuses on networking and conversations. Seeking out mentorship programs that are suited to your interests is a great way to expand your learning as a new teacher. The authors of this book feel passionately about the mentorship of new teachers that not only did we decide to write this book, we also wrote a mentorship book that compliments this work. In speaking with our good friend, Professor John Hattie, he explained the power of colleague to colleague mentorship. Meaning that seeking out other new teachers to hang out with and

share experiences is extremely valuable. We have included some online mentorship communities (listed at the end of this chapter) that you may want to explore!

GETTING THE MOST OUT OF PD OR PL

Just being honest here, there will be times in your career where you are not looking forward to your PD or PL session. As a matter of fact, you may be able to identify some coworkers who themselves are automatically resistant to the idea of new learning. This is an unfortunate reality of our job some days, after all we are all human and sometimes we just don't want to attend another meeting, PD, or PL session! With this reality aside, it is very easy to slip into the notion that all PD or PL is not valuable based upon a past experience. Please remember not all PD or PL is created equally, or presented to teachers equally and thus we must keep in mind the following notions in order to get the most out of our PD or PL experience.

- Sitting with friends and colleagues is great during these events, but be aware of their potential biases. It is very possible that if they have a negative view of the workshop it will impact your own experience. It is okay to be selfish and want to get the most out of these, so if that means sacrificing a seat with someone who may be too distracting, that's okay.
- If you are unfamiliar with the subject of the session, do a bit of research prior to attending. A simple google search, or a short YouTube video may be able to clarify some general information that will allow you to jump into the workshop without feeling lost from the onset.
- If the workshop you are attending is required by the district, ensure you are familiar with the key attributes being presented. Often these sessions are published on your district website, or available via email request.
- Take PD or PL at your own pace when possible. It is better to implement more slowly and more deliberately rather than try a new thing every week. It is very tempting to want to try everything you learned all at once, building our capacity as a practitioner is better suited when we implement in small chunks over a period of time rather than all at once.
- Implementation of new learning is slow, and arduous and requires care and grace. Ensure that you are implementing with care, meaning you understand the impact this implementation will have on your students.

Ensuring you are implementing with grace means understanding that not everything will go according to plan, and that's okay! Give yourself the opportunity to try, fail, refine, and retry.

Messy implementation is often the type of implementation that yields the best results.

Ultimately, the goal of your new learning is the residual impact it will have on your students, through the refinement of your already stellar teaching skills! Having a better understanding of the types of learning and development available to you will allow you to be more deliberate in determining which workshops you decide to attend. One invaluable truth that exists though is that as teachers we are never truly finished learning. Whether you have been teaching for 30 days or 30 years, PD and PL offers opportunities for us to continually learn about the latest in education as we continue to refine our practice.

QUESTIONS TO ASK YOUR MENTOR OR COLLEAGUES

1. Where can I find postings about upcoming PD or PL workshops available to me? How many of these are funded by the district vs. out of pocket?
2. What has been your most impactful PD or PL experience? What about this experience was so valuable for you?
3. Is there a body of research that you recommend considering the direction our school or district is heading with our teaching philosophy?

BRINGING IT ALL TOGETHER

The bread and butter of great teaching starts with a solid lesson design, and high-quality planning. Knowing how to plan and envision a path toward mastery for your students sets the foundation for all instructional and assessment practices (which we will discuss in later chapters). In many ways, the structure of your planning, whether collaborative, independent, or with the support of AI technologies, is not nearly as important as knowing where we are intending to lead our classrooms. This cannot be done by chance, but rather we must be intentional in the way we design our lessons.

While we could not include every aspect of planning and lesson design in this chapter, we wanted to include elements we wished we would have known about when we first started teaching. In essence, please take a lesson from Toolbox Tactic 4.6: Give yourself opportunities to try, fail, and refine. Taking on the responsibilities of planning and lesson design as a new teacher will be much more frustrating if you do not give yourself grace! Pick one or two of the toolbox tactics from this chapter and try them out! We have left a space on the next page for you to record your successes, and your new learning to track your progress over the course of your year. Good luck and happy planning!

IMPLEMENTATION TRACKER

<table>
<tr><td colspan="2">Attempted toolbox tactic:</td></tr>
<tr><td>Successes:</td><td>Roadblocks:</td></tr>
<tr><td colspan="2">What should I change to be more successful next time?</td></tr>
</table>

Attempted toolbox tactic:	
Successes:	Roadblocks:
What should I change to be more successful next time?	

5

SETTING THE STAGE: THE SIGNIFICANCE OF THE LEARNING ENVIRONMENT FOR STUDENT SUCCESS

As you step into the world of teaching, it's essential to recognize the pivotal role that the learning environment plays in shaping students' academic achievements, engagement, and overall well-being. In this section, we will explore why creating a conducive learning environment is crucial for fostering optimal learning outcomes for students, especially in your first few years of teaching.

UNDERSTANDING THE LEARNING ENVIRONMENT

The learning environment encompasses a myriad of factors that collectively influence students' learning experiences. It goes beyond the physical space to include social, emotional, and psychological elements. Research indicates that the learning environment significantly impacts students' cognitive development, motivation, and attitudes toward learning (Corno & Mandinach, 1983). For instance, classroom layout, lighting, temperature, and seating arrangements can profoundly affect students' concentration levels and academic performance (Tanner, 2009).

Furthermore, the social dynamics within the learning environment, such as peer interactions, teacher-student relationships, and collaborative learning opportunities, play a crucial role in fostering a sense of belonging and engagement among students (Hattie, 2009, 2023). Positive social interactions not only contribute to students' emotional well-being but also enhance their communication skills, critical thinking abilities, and problem-solving capabilities (Johnson & Johnson, 2014). Consider the following key elements of an effective learning environment.

KEY ELEMENTS OF AN EFFECTIVE LEARNING ENVIRONMENT

Physical Environment

A well-designed physical environment sets the stage for effective learning. It should be clean, organized, and aesthetically pleasing. Consider factors such as classroom layout, seating arrangements, lighting, and classroom decor. Additionally, integrating technology and multimedia resources can enhance learning experiences and facilitate interactive engagement.

Psychological Safety

Creating a psychologically safe environment where students feel accepted, respected, and supported is essential for promoting risk-taking and intellectual growth. Teachers play a vital role in cultivating trust and rapport by providing constructive feedback, encouraging open dialogue, and valuing diverse perspectives.

Cultural Relevance

Recognizing and honoring students' cultural backgrounds, identities, and experiences is critical for creating an inclusive learning environment. Incorporating culturally relevant curriculum materials, diverse perspectives, and multicultural pedagogies can foster a sense of belonging and empower students from marginalized communities.

Emotional Support

Addressing students' social-emotional needs and well-being is paramount for their overall development. Educators can implement strategies such as mindfulness practices, emotional regulation techniques, and counseling support to promote resilience, self-awareness, and empathy.

Engagement and Collaboration

Promoting active engagement, inquiry-based learning, and collaborative activities can stimulate students' curiosity, creativity, and critical thinking skills. By providing opportunities for hands-on experiences, group discussions, and project-based learning, educators can foster a dynamic and interactive learning environment.

WAYS TO ENHANCE THE LEARNING ENVIRONMENT

Creating an effective learning environment requires intentional effort and thoughtful planning. The purpose of this section is to offer different ways we may consider enhancing our learning environments. By all means, we will be providing some building blocks for you to consider in the next section of the chapter, yet we felt it would be pertinent to give more general ideas regarding making your classroom the best possible place for learning!

1. Classroom Design: Optimize the physical layout of the classroom to facilitate movement, interaction, and accessibility. Arrange furniture to promote collaboration and create designated learning spaces for different activities.

2. Positive Reinforcement: Provide positive reinforcement, praise, and recognition for students' efforts and achievements. Celebrate diversity and individual strengths to create a culture of appreciation and inclusivity.

3. Community Building: Implement team-building activities, icebreakers, and cooperative learning tasks to foster a sense of community and belonging among students. Encourage peer support and collaboration to promote empathy and mutual respect.

4. Flexibility and Differentiation: Recognize students' diverse learning styles, interests, and abilities, and offer flexible instructional approaches and differentiated assignments to accommodate individual needs. Personalize learning experiences to empower students to take ownership of their learning journey.

5. Reflective Practice: Engage in ongoing reflection and self-assessment to evaluate the effectiveness of teaching strategies and make adjustments to better meet students' needs. Seek feedback from students and colleagues to foster continuous improvement and innovation in the learning environment.

Creating a conducive learning environment is more than arranging desks and chairs; it's about cultivating a space where students feel valued, supported, and motivated to learn. By attending to the physical, social, emotional, and psychological dimensions of the learning environment, educators can create an atmosphere that fosters student growth, engagement, and success. As you explore the various building blocks presented below and as you navigate through these first few years, remember that the learning environment you create can have a profound impact on the success of your students.

As you embark through the rest of this chapter, we wanted to make sure you had a clear map of the concepts and ideas that will be explored more in depth. Like we mentioned previously in the introduction, do not feel pressured to try and apply all of these ideas, rather explore as many of these as you can and apply what piques your interests or needs. Enjoy exploring the following toolbox tactics:

1. Understanding Your Physical Classroom Environment: The way your classroom is setup communicates your desired intentions of student learning. By creating awareness of the environment as the third teacher we can design an optimal physical space for learning.
2. The Who Before You Do, Discover More About Your Students: Our instructional impact is predicated on how well we know our students. Taking time early on to learn about our students as humans will create better opportunities for instructional impact.
3. The Importance of Classroom Routines: Students thrive on routines, and in many cases a routine can mitigate other management issues. Establishing and reinforcing learning routines with students is importantly impactful.
4. Classroom Climate and Fostering An Environment of Mistakes: As important as the physical environment, the climate of our classrooms will impact the way our students learn.
5. Importance of Teacher Student Relationships: Balancing instructional delivery with students requires a delicate understanding of how we can foster positive teacher-student relationships in a classroom setting.
6. Creating a Brave Space: Psychological safety for students is equally important and physical safety. By creating a brave space we can ensure all students feel safe and welcome to learn.

TOOLBOX TACTIC 5.1 UNDERSTANDING YOUR PHYSICAL CLASSROOM ENVIRONMENT

Case: *You have just inherited your very own classroom space, and when you walk in it appears like it is just a pile of unorganized desks. What should you do? Rather than set up your classroom haphazardly, keep in mind that the classroom layout has a direct influence on the way your classroom will operate.*

From Vince: *Teaching social studies to high school students afforded me many opportunities to make the classroom space work for me. By organizing desks in certain ways (e.g., In pods for collaboration, in lines to represent political and economic spectrums), I promoted certain ways of thinking for my students. Do not underestimate the power of a well-organized physical space!*

You have likely heard the term *physical environment* a lot in your teacher preparation studies. What comes to mind when you hear it? You might think of the layout of a classroom space, how desks, tables, and resources are situated within a space, or even how student work displays and posters are used, but there is much more to consider. Have you ever heard someone claim that the classroom is "the third teacher?" As strange as this might sound, there is a lot of truth to this statement.

The phrase "the classroom environment is the third teacher" comes from the Reggio Emilia approach to early childhood education, which emphasizes the significant role that the environment plays in children's learning. In this context, the "first teacher" is the parent, the "second teacher" is you, the educator, and the "third teacher" is the physical environment of the classroom. This concept highlights how the environment itself can act as a powerful tool for learning and development. It is important to note that although this work was centered on early learning, the ideas of how your physical teaching space is situated impacts student learning at all levels.

THE THIRD TEACHER

So right now you are probably wondering, okay, the classroom space and how it is set up or decorated, for example, is important, but how is it the third teacher? Let's examine eight key ideas as to how your classroom can serve as the third teacher.

1. **Learning as an Interactive Process**
   The classroom environment is not just a backdrop for learning but an active participant in the educational process. It provides opportunities for students to explore, discover, and interact with materials and resources, facilitating self-directed learning.

2. **Encouraging Autonomy and Independence**
   A well-designed classroom environment encourages students to take initiative, make choices, and engage in activities independently. By organizing materials in accessible ways and creating inviting learning stations, the environment empowers students to take control of their learning.

3. **Fostering Collaboration and Social Interaction**
   The layout and organization of the classroom can promote collaboration and social learning. For example, arranging desks in clusters encourages group work, while designated areas for different activities can foster peer interaction and cooperative learning.

4. **Stimulating Curiosity and Imagination**
   The environment can inspire curiosity and creativity through the use of diverse materials, interactive displays, and spaces that invite exploration. A thoughtfully curated environment can provoke questions, spark ideas, and encourage students to engage in creative problem-solving.

5. **Supporting Different Learning Styles**
   The classroom environment can be designed to accommodate various learning styles and needs. By offering a range of spaces—quiet corners for reading, open areas for movement, and sensory-rich materials—the environment can support visual, auditory, kinesthetic, and other types of learners.

6. **Reflecting Cultural and Individual Diversity**
   The environment can be a reflection of the students' cultural backgrounds and individual identities. By incorporating diverse materials, books, and displays, the classroom becomes a space where all students feel seen and valued, which can enhance their sense of belonging and engagement.

7. **Creating a Sense of Safety and Well-being**
   A well-organized and aesthetically pleasing environment can contribute to students' emotional and psychological well-being. When students feel safe, comfortable, and welcomed in their physical surroundings, they are more likely to engage positively with learning.

8. **Continuous Learning and Adaptation**
   The environment is dynamic and evolves based on the needs and interests of the students. Teachers can adapt the physical space to align with the current curriculum, projects, or the development of specific skills, making the environment a living, responsive element of the learning process.

When we consider all of these together, we realize that referring to the classroom environment as the third teacher really means that how we set up our classroom influences student interaction with knowledge, each other, and the world around them. The environment is seen not just as a passive setting but as an active, intentional, and responsive part of the learning process. So, beyond having displays, posters, and a cool desk arrangement, how does one go about leveraging their classroom as the third teacher? Let's find out!

MAKING MY CLASSROOM THE THIRD TEACHER

For you, a new teacher aiming to make your classroom the third teacher, the physical environment should be thoughtfully designed to actively support your students' learning experiences. Here are three effective ways that you can achieve this.

1. **Create Flexible Learning Spaces**
   - Design a classroom layout that can be easily rearranged to suit different learning activities and styles. Include various zones for different purposes—such as a reading corner, collaborative workstations, a quiet area for individual work, and open space for hands-on activities or movement.
   - **How It Works:** Flexible spaces allow students to choose environments that best suit their learning preferences and the task at hand. For example, students might use the quiet area for independent reading or the collaborative workstations for group projects. By adapting the physical environment to meet the needs of diverse learners and activities, the classroom becomes an active participant in the educational process.
2. **Incorporate Student-Centered Displays and Resources**
   - Use classroom walls, bulletin boards, and other display areas to showcase student work, learning resources, and interactive materials that are relevant to the current curriculum and student interests.

- **How It Works:** When students see their work displayed, it validates their efforts and makes the classroom feel like a shared space where their contributions are valued. Interactive displays, such as word walls, question boards, or thematic corners, invite students to engage with the content regularly. This not only reinforces learning but also encourages exploration and curiosity, making the environment a key player in the learning process.

3. **Implement an Accessible and Organized Materials System**
   - Organize classroom materials and resources in a way that is easily accessible to students. Use labeled bins, shelves, and stations so that students can independently find and use the tools they need for various tasks.
   - **How It Works:** When materials are organized and easily accessible, students are empowered to take ownership of their learning. They can gather supplies, choose activities, and clean up independently, which fosters responsibility and autonomy. This also allows the environment to function as a third teacher by enabling seamless transitions between activities and encouraging students to explore different resources on their own.

These three approaches help create an environment that not only supports but also actively enhances student learning, making the physical classroom a dynamic and integral part of the educational experience.

KEY TAKEAWAY

Beginning teachers should aim to create a classroom environment that is organized, inclusive, flexible, and conducive to learning. This involves thoughtful planning, ongoing reflection, and a willingness to adapt the physical space to meet the needs of all students. To reinforce our understanding of this, let's read a story about a new teacher, Torry, who was struggling with how to set up the classroom to maximize student engagement.

SCHOOL STORIES

Torry Pines for Help!

Torry had always dreamed of being a teacher, and now, fresh out of college, was about to begin the first year as a fifth-grade teacher. The excitement was palpable, but so was the anxiety. Having spent countless hours preparing lesson plans, there was still one thing that kept Torry up at night: the classroom set-up.

No matter how hard Torry tried, the arrangement of desks and learning stations just didn't seem right. They wanted the room to be inviting and conducive to learning, but every time they moved a desk or shifted a shelf, something still felt off.

After a few fitful days of frustration, Torry finally decided to reach out to Chris, a mentor teacher, who had years of experience and a knack for creating engaging classroom environments.

Chris arrived after school one day, with a warm smile and a coffee in hand. "I hear you've been having some trouble with the set-up," Chris stated, glancing around the room.

Torry nodded, feeling a bit embarrassed. "I've tried everything, but nothing seems to work. The room just doesn't feel right. I bought a lot of literacy and numeracy poster and such but . . . I don't know . . ."

Chris took a slow walk around the room, considering the space. Chris asked Torry about the goals for the classroom—how Torry wanted the students to interact, where Torry envisioned group work happening, and the plans to use the different areas of the room.

After listening carefully, Chris offered some simple yet profound advice. "Think of your classroom like a living thing. It's going to change and grow with your students. Start with the basics—a clear path for movement, a cozy reading nook, and spaces where kids can work together or independently. Don't be afraid to experiment and change things as the year goes on."

With Chris's guidance, Torry rearranged the desks into small clusters to encourage collaboration and moved the reading corner to a sunny spot by the window. Torry created a flexible space at the back of the room for hands-on activities and set up a welcoming area near the door where students could leave their things and feel at home.

As they stood back to admire the new layout, Torry felt a sense of relief and excitement. The room felt different—alive, ready to be filled with the energy of curious fifth graders.

"Thank you, Chris," Torry said, with a grateful smile.

"Anytime," Chris replied, giving Torry a reassuring pat on the back. "Remember, the best classrooms aren't perfect—they're adaptable. The classroom is also the third teacher! Let it help you to help the students with their learning. You've got this."

And with that, Torry felt ready for the new school year, confident that the classroom space would be ready to grow, learn, and adapt along with the students.

REFLECTIVE PRACTICE

Have you felt similar feelings as Torry? Think about the classroom or learning spaces where you are going to be teaching. Envision how you might want to arrange or rearrange desks, tables and centers. You could also take some time to measure the space, consider lighting, technology set-up, and accessibility of teaching materials and tools.

Make a sketch or mock-up of the space and play with your ideas. Think about the learning needs of your students. Do some require less stimulation? Do some need a quiet learning corner? Do you have a variety of flexible work and learning areas? Where will you display student work to showcase and celebrate their successes? Like Torry, we encourage you to connect with a mentor, teacher, or trusted colleague to share ideas.

QUESTIONS TO ASK YOUR MENTOR OR COLLEAGUES

Here are three questions you could ask your mentor teacher about how the classroom can serve as the third teacher:

1. How can the physical arrangement and design of my classroom environment support and enhance student learning and engagement?
2. What tools and approaches might you recommend I use to make my classroom environment reflect the school's educational philosophy and support the diverse needs of our students?
3. How might I incorporate student input in shaping the classroom environment to ensure it evolves as a dynamic space that promotes curiosity and exploration?

TOOLBOX TACTIC 5.2 THE WHO BEFORE YOU DO, DISCOVER MORE ABOUT YOUR STUDENTS

Case: *Managing 20+ students on a daily basis (or in the case of the secondary teachers . . . per class) can be a daunting task. Often the way we teach is the preferred way we learned when we were in the classroom. Think about your* *favorite teacher growing up, chances are you are trying to mimic them because they had such a profound impact on you. While there is nothing wrong with this, there is a chance you are missing out on impacting some of your own students. So take the time. Take the time to learn about them as little human beings and use that information to influence the way you teach.*

From Wayne*: Early in my career, I spent a lot of time in the local RecPlex playing a variety of sports and got to see a number of my students doing what they loved. They were always more than happy to see me in the stands cheering them on and it always seemed to result in better relationships with them in the classroom. Thus, if I ever got an invitation from a student and their family to come watch them play a sport, act in a play, dance in a recital, or whatever, I have gone. Thus, I have watched water polo, synchronized swimming, bowling matches, piano recitals, dance competitions, and a host of other things and each time it brought me closer to my students and their families as people.*

SCHOOL STORIES

Ms. Canter

It's the first day of classes at Valley Mountain Middle School and Ms. Amanda Canter is excited for her second year as a teacher. She recently moved to middle school from teaching third grade last year, and the transition to middle school has been tough. But overall, she is very excited about teaching the seventh grade. She was able to prepare for a content heavy course over a few weeks thanks to her grade-level partners who took time out of their summer vacation to meet with her and share their resources. As the bell rings for the first block of the day, Ms. Canter is nervous but excited. "Class please take your seats; we are going to review the class procedures and jump right into the book. We have a lot to do today, and a lot of information to cover this semester so let's get to it!" Students quickly straighten in their seats and look around trying to figure out if their teacher is serious or not.

Does this story sound familiar? Perhaps you have done something similar or experienced something like that as a student yourself. The reality of this situation is that the first few years of teaching are INTENSE, that's no lie. We are inundated with scheduling, planning, grading, cleaning, emailing . . . what feels like an endless list of all the things we try to do on a daily and weekly basis. On top of that, we are also tasked with teaching students! Managing it all can really feel like a situation where we find ourselves saying "I just have soooo much to do." Have you said that to yourself already? Well, you aren't alone, we all have—many, many times. We know the classroom is a busy place and sometimes we feel like jumping into the lesson as soon as possible, however; this may not be the best course of action. We strongly advocate that at the beginning of the year you learn about your students before diving into what can feel like an insurmountable amount of content. Another way to think about this, is to consider the WHO in your class before you DO any instruction.

Make time to learn about who your students are as *people*. What are their interests outside of the classroom? What passions do they have? What are they good at outside of the classroom (something you wouldn't know by only seeing them in the class)?

What gifts, talents, or perspectives do your students have that would enhance the learning environment for all other students and you as well?

Professor John Hattie refers to this as the skill, will, and thrill of the learner and in Figure 5.1 we will unpack that means (Hattie & Donoghue, 2016).

5.1 The Skill, Will, and Thrill of a Learner

Skill	The skill refers to the prior knowledge and experiences the students carry with them that can impact their classroom learning. This prior knowledge can come from previous learning through other grades, interests, and hobbies, and even aspects of them as a person that we may not know, unless we ask. An example of this would be whether the student speaks another language; this influences the way they perceive learning.
Will	The will refers to the specific dispositions' students have inherently in their personality. Dispositions reflect how the learner responds to learning situations that are challenging or new to them. Certain learners who hold specific dispositions toward learning may be more willing to persist in challenging times, whereas other students may seek collaboration (an example of a disposition) to help them in challenging situations.
Thrill	The thrill refers to a learner's motivation, and reasons why they engage in the classroom experience. When the thrill of learning is higher, often students will perceive that learning was enjoyable and did not require effort. It is not that the task is easy, but rather they were motivated to accomplish a task and engage in the learning.

There are many ways you can engage in a discovery process with your students, but the most important thing is to be deliberate in making time to do this. Ensuring we know who the students are in our class will help us make more accurate decisions about how to teach them and in turn will maximize the impact of our instruction. It may feel like you are sacrificing valuable instructional time but trust us when we say that by taking these steps early you will gain that time back later in the school year. Figure 5.2 shows a few simple ways to engage in the discovery process with your students.

5.2 Different Ways to Discover More About Our Students

Entrance Tickets	Not unlike exit tickets, these are low stakes opportunities to discover more about students' skills, and prior knowledge regarding a topic or unit of study.
Tell Me More	Give your students the opportunity to tell you more about themselves. Have the submit a video response or voice note, e.g., telling you more about them as a person. This is a great opportunity for them to tell you about their life outside of school. You will be surprised at what you learn!
Attend School Events	This may sound obvious but trust us, attend when you can! Also, make sure you attend events outside of your interests: if you are an athletic person, attend a band concert, art show, or year play; if athletics are not your thing, attend a school sporting event. You will be shocked at what your students are capable of when you see them in their comfort zone.
Student-Generated Questions	Prior to engaging in instruction of new content, present your students with a "preview" of the content and allow them to generate as many questions as possible for you. You will begin to see where their understanding of the content is according to what you need to teach them.

(Continued)

(Continued)

Teacher Noticing	Teacher noticing is a process of being hyper-observant when students are engaging in a particular task or activity. More than observing however, the teacher should be reflective and interpretive on what they noticed. What information can we glean from our observations that can help us learn more about our students' skill, will, and thrill.

There are many other ways to engage in the discovery process, but we wanted to provide you with a few actions you could take immediately. One thing we haven't mentioned yet, is the impact this process has on the development of the relationships you have with your students. The bottom line is students notice when their teacher takes an interest in them as people. They know when you attend their game, art show, concert, speech and debate event, for example, and that also has positive impacts on your teaching.

QUESTIONS TO ASK YOUR MENTOR OR COLLEAGUES

1. Does your school have a calendar of major events where students can display their talents you may not see in your own classroom? (A calendar will help you plan ahead.)
2. What strategies does your mentor have to continue to add to your discovery strategy toolbox?

REFLECTIVE PRACTICE

Think about how you are intending on engaging in a "re-discovery process." At the beginning of a new unit of study or major shift in content, how might you engage in a discovery process to learn about your students and their prior knowledge regarding that topic? (Hint: Sometimes the discovery process can be a review from your previous instruction!)

TOOLBOX TACTIC 5.3 THE IMPORTANCE OF CLASSROOM ROUTINES

Case: *Have you ever tried to explain your morning routine to a friend? From what time you wake up, to having that first (or second) cup of coffee and then making your way to work, we tend to be creatures of habit. Simply stated, we like routines. So do your students! Routines offer structure and familiarity. Routines help our students to settle into their learning and can provide them with greater levels of focus and attentiveness to learning tasks. How good is that!*

From Vince: *When I first started, I knew my routines but never took the time to coach my students about the class routines. In fact, I had just assumed that the students knew the routines based on the fact that they had been in school already. Boy was I wrong, It was not until I started writing the class agenda on the board that I saw a difference in my students. They started expecting to see the agenda written on the board and once they saw it, they adjusted themselves accordingly. The routine helped my students, as well as myself get mentally ready for the teaching and learning of the day.*

In your growth as a new teacher, you have heard many important ideas about having a greater impact in your teaching practice. Classroom management and time management are two common areas of inquiry that you, like so many new teachers, have wondered about. We want our students to engage in their learning to the greatest extent possible and we know that there is a lot of content to cover in the curricula. Thus, we need to become better at making the most of the instructional time we have. Routines, as you will see, can really help you to manage the flow and quality of learning that takes place.

The great news is routines, which are a form of deliberate practice, help us to establish a classroom environment that gives students the structures and supports they need to be more engaged in their learning. So, let's explore seven big ideas why classroom routines are so worthy of your consideration. Have a look at Figure 5.3.

5.3 The Benefits of Routines

Benefit	Importance
Creates a Predictable Environment	Routines help students know what to expect, reducing anxiety and helping them focus on learning. When students understand the flow of the day, they can better anticipate what comes next, which enhances their comfort and security in the classroom.
Maximizes Instructional Time	Efficient routines minimize downtime and transition chaos, allowing more time for actual instruction. When students know the procedures for entering the classroom, starting assignments, and transitioning between activities, less time is wasted.
Promotes Classroom Management	Clear routines help maintain order by setting expectations for behavior. When students know the routine for things like raising their hands, lining up, or how to seek help, it reduces disruptions and fosters a positive learning environment.
Supports Student Independence	Routines empower students to manage themselves and their work with minimal teacher intervention. This encourages them to take responsibility for their learning, leading to greater independence and confidence.
Facilitates a Positive Learning Environment	Consistent routines contribute to a calm and organized atmosphere, which is conducive to learning. They help in building a classroom culture where students feel respected and understood, as everyone knows the expectations.
Helps in Differentiating Instruction	Routines allow teachers to manage the classroom efficiently, making it easier to implement differentiated instruction and meet individual student needs.
Assists in Managing Diverse Needs	For students with special needs or those who require additional support, predictable routines are particularly beneficial. They provide a stable framework that can help these students thrive.

So, now that we have considered some of the benefits, let's take a look at some routines that have been found to be very useful for new teachers. Please note that these can be used (adapted or modified) for both elementary and secondary students.

1. **Morning and Beginning of Class Routines**
   - **Greeting at the Door:** Welcoming each student with a greeting sets a positive tone for the day and establishes a connection.
   - **The First Five:** Use the first five minutes of your class or day to establish the nonnegotiable routines (attendance, lesson set up, etc.). The truth is there are a lot of "teacher things" that need to be done, predictably taking the first five minutes of the day or lesson will create those necessary routines for students.
   - **Morning Work:** Assigning a simple task like journaling, silent reading, or a review activity helps students transition into the learning mindset as soon as they enter the classroom.
   - **Attendance:** Incorporating student jobs like taking attendance or managing the lunch count fosters responsibility.
2. **Transition Routines**
   - **Signal for Attention:** Using a specific sound, phrase, or hand signal to get students' attention quickly is effective for smooth transitions.
   - **Lining Up:** Teaching students to line up in a specific order or according to a pattern (like height or alphabetical order) helps maintain order during transitions.
   - **Rotation Between Centers:** Clear instructions and a visual timer for rotating between different learning stations or centers help minimize chaos and maximize learning time.
3. **Classroom Management Routines**
   - **Behavior Expectations:** Implementing a consistent system, such as a color-coded chart or a point system, helps students understand the consequences of their behavior.
   - **"Do Now" Activities:** Starting each lesson with a brief, focused activity related to the lesson topic helps students settle in and focus quickly.
   - **Quiet Signals:** A visual or auditory signal (like raising a hand or flicking the lights) can be used to quickly bring the class to silence.

4. **Instructional Routines**
   - **Daily Agenda:** Posting the day's schedule or objectives on the board helps students know what to expect and stay on task.
   - **Interactive Read-Aloud:** Incorporating regular read-aloud sessions with opportunities for student participation fosters engagement and comprehension.
   - **Exit Tickets:** At the end of a lesson, using exit tickets with questions related to the lesson helps assess understanding and informs future instruction.
5. **Classroom Organization Routines**
   - **Desk or Supply Checks:** Regularly scheduled times for students to organize their desks and supplies encourage responsibility and reduce clutter.
   - **Materials Distribution:** Designating a student helper or setting up a system for distributing and collecting materials efficiently minimizes disruptions.
   - **Homework Routine:** Establishing a consistent routine for assigning, collecting, and reviewing homework helps students develop responsibility and keeps them on track.
6. **End-of-Day Routines**
   - **Classroom Cleanup:** Assigning roles for end-of-day cleanup teaches students to take care of their environment.
   - **Review of the Day:** A quick discussion or reflection on what was learned during the day reinforces key concepts and helps students feel a sense of accomplishment.
   - **Packing Up:** A structured routine for packing up, including reminders for homework and notes to parents, ensures that students leave the classroom organized and prepared for the next day.
7. **Community Building Routines**
   - **Morning Meetings:** Starting the day with a brief meeting where students can share news, discuss goals, or address classroom concerns fosters a sense of community and belonging.
   - **Classroom Jobs:** Rotating jobs like line leader, board cleaner, or paper passer helps students take ownership of the classroom and learn responsibility.

- **Positive Reinforcement:** Regularly recognizing positive behavior through praise, rewards, or a classroom recognition system helps build a supportive classroom culture.

These routines, when consistently applied, help create a stable environment where students know what is expected, feel secure, and can focus on learning. As a new teacher remember that establishing and maintaining effective routines can ease your transition into teaching, help you manage your classroom effectively and focus on delivering quality instruction.

THE POWER OF WELCOMING ROUTINES

One area that I (Tim) feel has perhaps the greatest impact on helping students get off to a great start each day are your welcoming routines. Most of the routines I share next are great for welcoming your students in the morning. This is perhaps the most important time of the school day as you can truly get a sense of how your students are feeling, for example, tired, sad, or happy. We know that we as teachers might feel these too (especially if we didn't get our coffee) and by establishing routines that allow for a quick check-in prior to class, you can really gain a sense of what socioemotional support a student might need. Allow me to share a story with you about a dear colleague who, in my humble opinion, was one of the very best models of effective greeting techniques.

SCHOOL STORIES

The Remarkable Mr. Robson

Greg Robson started his teaching career in a small, seaside town in Newfoundland and Labrador (Canada). He moved to British Columbia for a few years to teach in another small seaside town and then made his way to a rural northern Alberta village where I first met him. I (Tim) was in the early years of my teaching career and, given that Greg had several more years of teaching experience, he became a rich resource (a mentor) to me.

(Continued)

(Continued)

What I appreciated about Greg was how he greeted every one of his students at the door. This was not just a "Hi, nice to see you" greeting, it was a level of getting to know something great about each student, about building a relationship. He would know what teams they cheered for, what hobbies and interests they had, what music or movies excited them. Knowing I was a new teacher, Greg encouraged me to try a similar routine. I leveraged humor, fun handshakes, trivia questions, and fun facts into my welcoming routines and soon found myself getting to know the students at a deeper level. Greg and I often attended local sporting events and cultural activities whereby the students realized that we took interest in them beyond the classroom. Parents and community members noted this too and by establishing this level of rapport, it became easier when having to tend to difficult or challenging situations. I eventually moved to a larger center to teach but Greg and I kept in touch.

Fast forward eight years later: I was an assistant principal at a large Grade 7-12 school. We needed a math teacher and counselor. I contacted Greg to tell him about the opportunity. Following an interview, my principal welcomed Greg to our staff. In short order, Greg became well known on campus for how quickly he not only learned the names of his students, but the entire campus!

Each morning, without fail, Greg would stand in the corridor about a half hour before class start up, to welcome students as they entered the building. He would introduce himself, tell a fun fact and over the period of a few weeks would learn names, grade level, and something about each student. As a counselor, this was his superpower. Eventually, I became principal and was always so taken, so impressed with Greg's morning ritual.

Greg took his morning routine very seriously and it was wonderful to witness how he would take time to learn traditional greetings of all the diverse languages and cultures within our learning community. He would start by offering his favorite Newfoundland greetings and then invite students to teach him how to say good morning, have a great day, how was your weekend, have a great weekend, thank goodness it's Friday, and other similar sayings. Soon, Greg would be greeting and bantering in over 40 different languages! He was revered by students, staff and families for how he made the time to greet everyone by name, in their custom, and with a fun fact or story that helped lift everyone's spirit at the start of each day. Other teachers, just like me years earlier, looked to the example set by Greg, and added a meaningful morning welcoming of students, parents, and staff as a part of their daily routine.

SOME WAYS TO ADD TO YOUR MORNING ROUTINES

Here are some good welcoming routines that new teachers can use:

1. **Greeting at the Door**: Stand at the door and greet each student by name with a smile, a greeting in their home language, a handshake, fist bump, or high five. This creates a personal connection and makes students feel valued.
2. **Morning Meeting**: Start the day with a brief meeting where students can share something about themselves, discuss the plan for the day, or engage in a short team-building activity. This builds community and helps students transition into the school day.
3. **Question of the Day**: Display a fun or thought-provoking question on the board as students enter the classroom. Encourage them to write their answers on a sticky note and place it on a chart or whiteboard. This sparks conversation and engages students right from the start.
4. **Do Now/Bell Ringer Activity**: Have a quick, engaging task ready for students as they enter the classroom, such as a warm-up question, a journal prompt, or a quick review problem. This helps students settle in and focus on learning immediately.
5. **Positive Affirmations:** Start the day with a few minutes of positive affirmations. Students can repeat a class affirmation or create their own. This fosters a positive mindset and encourages self-confidence.
6. **Music and Calm Start:** Play calming or upbeat music as students enter the room. This can create a welcoming atmosphere and help set the tone for the day.
7. **Classroom Jobs Rotation:** Assign daily or weekly classroom jobs and rotate them regularly. As students enter, they can check their job for the day, which gives them a sense of responsibility and ownership in the classroom.
8. **Daily Goal Setting**: Encourage students to set a personal or academic goal for the day. They can share their goals with a partner or write them down in a designated space. This promotes reflection and motivation.

9. **Compliment Circle**: Once a week, start the day with a compliment circle where students take turns giving a compliment to a classmate. This fosters kindness and helps build a supportive classroom environment.

10. **Class Motto or Chant:** Develop a class motto, chant, or cheer that students recite together at the beginning of each day. This builds unity and sets a positive tone for the day ahead. These routines help create a structured and supportive environment where students feel welcomed and ready to learn.

MINDFUL REMINDERS

Classroom routines are generally beneficial for creating a structured and predictable learning environment, but they can have potential pitfalls if not implemented thoughtfully. Here are some possible pitfalls:

- **Overreliance on Routines**: Strict adherence to routines can lead to a lack of flexibility. This can make it difficult to adapt to unexpected situations or to accommodate diverse learning needs.
- **Stifling Creativity**: If routines are too rigid, they can suppress creativity and spontaneity, both for students and teachers. Students may become too focused on following procedures rather than thinking critically or creatively.
- **Routine Fatigue**: Students might become bored or disengaged if the same routines are used every day without variation. This can lead to a decrease in motivation and enthusiasm for learning.
- **Lack of Student Buy-In**: If students don't understand the purpose of a routine or see it as arbitrary, they may resist following it, which can create classroom management issues.
- **Inflexibility in Response to Individual Needs**: Routines that are too uniform may not accommodate students with different learning styles, abilities, or needs. This can lead to some students feeling left out or struggling to keep up.
- **Teacher Dependence**: Teachers might become overly dependent on routines, leading to a lack of responsiveness to

the dynamics of the classroom. This can result in missed opportunities for teachable moments or adjustments based on student needs.

- **Routine Implementation Without Reflection:** Without periodic reflection and adjustment, routines can become outdated or ineffective. Teachers need to regularly assess whether routines are still meeting their intended goals and make changes as needed.

Routines can add great value to classroom management and more effective use of instructional time. Balancing consistency with flexibility, and regularly reflecting on the effectiveness of routines, can help you mitigate these potential pitfalls and maximize student engagement in their learning.

QUESTIONS TO ASK YOUR MENTOR OR COLLEAGUES

1. What are the most essential routines to establish at the beginning of the school year?
2. What should I do if students struggle to follow established routines?
3. Can you share some examples of routines that have worked well for you?
4. How can I ensure that my routines are developmentally appropriate for my students?

TOOLBOX TACTIC 5.4 CLASSROOM CLIMATE AND FOSTERING AN ENVIRONMENT OF MISTAKES

Case: *Understanding the impact the environment of your classroom has on student learning is very important. In thinking about all aspects of our classrooms, we often forget to consider the climate of our classroom. What might be those intangible elements we can control that will in the long run prove to benefit our students and their learning experiences?*

From Wayne: *Over my career, there have been a number of triumphs with students and staff. However, I would be remiss if I did not admit*

(Continued)

(Continued)

that there has also been my fair share of failures and "course corrections." What I am proud to say is that the vast majority of those mistakes I made as a teacher and school leader were celebrated publicly by me in an attempt to normalize making mistakes. Early on, I recognized the value of making it okay to make a mistake, learn from it and grow. It also did a great deal to stop the development of a community that hides or feels ashamed when a mistake happens.

The intangible aspects of our classroom environment are equally, if not more important than the physical environment. When our classroom climate is harsh, students have more difficulty learning and progressing regardless of who they are. Aside from the physical environment (which was covered in another toolbox tactic), the classroom climate refers to the emotional, social, and intellectual conditions in which students learn. As new teachers who are looking to create a lasting impact on our students' learning, there is no better place to start than by establishing a classroom climate that fosters growth and learning. Here are a few ideas to consider to jumpstart a positive classroom environment:

Recognize all learners as unique humans with their own experiences. This is expanded more so in Toolbox Tactic 5.5, but overall it is so important to make connections to students in a place where students feel comfortable. For example, if you as the teacher are more inclined to sports and athletics, it is possible that you may be missing deeper connections with students who are arts focused. Meeting students where they are includes discovering more about their interests.

Recognize all learners come to us with unique dispositions. From an instructional standpoint, it may seem obvious to state that not all learners are comfortable learning the way you comfortably teach. Some students are more collaborative, and some students prefer to sit back and learn individually and the trick is determining what dispositions students have and may need to further develop. We recommend asking your students the following two questions:

- What type of environment allows you to thrive as a learner?
- What type of environment is less comfortable for your learning?

Once you take the responses into account, we recommend designing learning experiences that build upon the existing dispositions and fosters growth of the less comfortable dispositions.

Communicate the truth about learning to your students. At the end of the day, our students deserve to know that learning is supposed to be challenging, and it is okay to find classes difficult. Part of the learning process is celebrating when students have worked through challenges to consolidate their learning. Many times, teachers assume students know this, but communicating it deliberately will help students understand the value of the challenge.

Check your biases and sometimes your attitude! Oof! This one may seem a bit direct, but we promise it is well intentioned! What we mean by this is that you are human, and as a human you are bound to have good and bad days. Make sure you are giving yourself grace, and be okay with being less than 100 percent some times. On the days where you don't quite feel yourself, we recommend being transparent with your students. Quite honestly, the students can generally tell whether you are a bit off or not, but by being honest and transparent with this encourages students to do the same or at the very least feel comfortable also having an off day.

FOSTERING A MISTAKE FRIENDLY CLIMATE

Our students are so prone to feeling like they have to be perfect that often just the idea of making a mistake causes unnecessary anxiety. This begs the notion as to how we as teachers can ensure that our classrooms are places where it is okay to make mistakes and be human. This is further evidenced when we ask our students what they think being a "good student" means to them. Their responses are more often than not related to behaviors and discipline, and rarely do our students mention making mistakes as part of being a good learner. Let's explore a few ways we can make our classroom climate more friendly to mistakes.

Normalize mistakes in the classroom. This includes having an open conversation with students about the importance of mistakes in the learning process. Included in these conversations can be examples of "famous mistakes: and how they helped advance our society. Explain how mistakes have made you into the wonderful teacher you are today!

Include mistakes as a part of learning. It is important to understand the impact you have as the expert in the classroom. Regardless of whether you feel like it or not, your students look up to you as the expert and as such it is imperative that you share your expertise.

What we mean by this is as follows, as you model your lesson to your students be sure to include mistakes as part of the instruction. Talk to your students about how experts often make mistakes. When teaching your students explain to them how experts use previous mistakes to help navigate their way through their learning the next time. Also, when modeling, be sure to include examples that have mistakes embedded within them. Show and share practical ways to navigate through mistakes.

Fostering a positive classroom climate and an environment where mistakes are welcomed is not something that will occur as a by-product, rather this must be a move that is established deliberately. This means that you as the teacher should include aspects of this in your classroom routines and practices. The following excerpt from Ms. Shepherd highlights the importance of this.

VOICES FROM THE FIELD

Fostering and Environment of Mistakes

Hannah Shepherd

> *Learn the content—Teach the content—Stay organized—Engage students—Provide feedback—Establish community—Document learning—Differentiate—Communicate with parents.*

The list of expectations when working in a teaching role is lengthy and multifaceted. With everything that contributes to the mental load of this job, there are bound to be moments where you make a misstep, causing things to not go as planned. The ability to accept the mistakes you make and to grow from them are vital skills to develop as a teacher. Coincidentally, it is also one of the most important skills for you to instill in your students.

As a new teacher, I have been forced to become comfortable with the uncomfortable reality that I have made mistakes, and will continue to make mistakes. There have been lessons I have taught, realizing afterward that I had misunderstood the strategy, leaving my students with a gap in their understanding. There have been moments where I let my emotions take over during tricky interactions with students. There were times when I missed a deadline or failed to follow through on a responsibility. Though these moments are disheartening and uncomfortable, the teaching profession almost requires you to fail before you can succeed.

In the classroom, accepting the reality of mistakes is not limited to teachers. We ask our students every day to stretch themselves, to go out on a limb and engage in learning that is new to them. We want them to know and believe that when they fail, we, their teachers, are there to acknowledge them and provide what they need in order to walk away from that mistake with dignity as well as new understanding. As an educator, if you want to invite genuine participation from your students, they need to feel safe with you, and safe with each other. You can spark this connection by creating opportunities to build community in your classroom such as team-building games, morning meetings, class discussions, and SEL learning lessons. I feel strongly, however, that the most effective way to make mistakes feel better to the students is to make them yourself—and let the kids watch.

Though it took some intentionality at first, I'm finding it more and more natural to make personal mistakes I make in the classroom glaringly obvious to the students. I admit to the class that I have lost something, for example, or perhaps that I had become too upset and should not have. I tell anecdotes of my mistakes and missteps and accept feedback from the kids when I realize something needs to change. When students see a person that they hold in high regard as imperfect, they feel safer to be imperfect themselves.

At some point in the last four years of teaching, I came across the concept of "the perfect mistake" which is the idea that you've made exactly the mistake you were meant to, and that something positive will come from it. This phrase has become a constant in my dialogue with students—to see a problem as an opportunity to become better.

QUESTIONS TO ASK YOUR MENTOR OR COLLEAGUES

1. What are some examples of activities or lessons you have delivered that help students understand the value of mistakes?
2. How do you try your best to hide your biases from your students?

TOOLBOX TACTIC 5.5 IMPORTANCE OF TEACHER-STUDENT RELATIONSHIPS

Case: *Walking into a new classroom when you are a new student is tough. It's not easy as a teacher either. Relationships are the*

(Continued)

(Continued)

foundation for everything we do in our classrooms, but how do you magically create meaningful relationships with your students? The short answer is you can't but have hope, as there are things you can do to set the stage for those relationships to grow.

From Tim: *First impressions are lasting. Having taught in a northern community for my first few years in the profession, I moved to a larger suburban school district in southern Alberta where a new school was opening. I was a new teacher again in a community new to me. What helped me most with the transition was the skills I had learned in getting to know students in a context outside of the classroom. In inquiring about their hobbies, interests, and favorite music and in taking genuine interest in them, their first impression of me was My teacher wants to get to know me." It was thus easier to engage them in my instructional practice. Knowing a little bit about the "Who before we do" builds rapport, respect, and trust. It is true when we hear the expression "Relationships are everything!"*

One of the most enjoyable and fulfilling aspects of teaching is the interactions you will have with your students. However, it must also be mentioned that some of the most trying, heart wrenching moments in your career will be the relationships with those same students. Over the course of an average teacher career, there will be hundreds of young people who come and go through your learning space, each leave their mark, some more pronounced than others.

When we talk about our origin story, the reason we got into education there is always at least one educator who is central to the plot. Perhaps they were your favorite teacher or a coach or the director of the school production. But there they are and you remember them. Hopefully you will use them as a model for some of your teaching behaviors. But just as with any story there are always contrasts, and as such there may also be some in your story that are more of the cautionary tale variety, the ones you will strive to not be like. And the deciding factor in how you see these contrasts most likely relates back to how they treated you, your friends or other kids you may not have known but watched as they raised them up or put them down.

No doubt positive teacher-student relationships are important to building learning space environments that encourage and inspire. These relationships play a crucial role in students' academic and personal development, influencing their attitudes toward learning, motivation, and overall well-being. When students feel valued and understood by their teachers, they are more likely to engage in their studies and school life in general (Hattie, 2023). This sense of connection makes students feel safe in expressing their thoughts, asking questions, and being vulnerable in front of their peers and you. In turn, this enhances their academic performance and deepens their understanding of what you are teaching.

It is also well known that showing some interest in a student, saying hello and smiling, has a positive effect on a student's well-being. Teachers who show empathy, provide constructive feedback, and encourage their students help them develop a growth mindset. This mindset is necessary for students to overcome challenges, keep on when facing difficulties, and work to achieve their goals inside and outside the classroom.

Relationship building by teachers also contributes to the emotional and social development of students. A teacher can be a crucial source of guidance, helping students to navigate the complexities of school life and their own personal experiences. Appropriate teacher-student relationships can reduce feelings of anxiety and stress, promoting better mental health. Positive relationships can also influence classroom management. Students who respect and feel connected to their teachers are more likely to behave in a positive manner while those who feel belittled or ignored may not simply comply and behave for behavior's sake, instead contributing to problems in the classroom space. Classrooms with positive environments tend to be places where teachers are able to dedicate more time to instruction rather than discipline which is a good thing for everyone.

SCHOOL STORIES

Mr. Hanson sat across from Ms. Harbez, his mentor, in the faculty lounge, his brow furrowed with confusion. "Something strange happened in my third period today," he began. "We were reviewing a couple of formulas, and out of nowhere, one of my students, Andi, started making some critical comments to the class about how I was teaching. It wasn't just a simple complaint; it felt personal!"

Ms. Harbez listened attentively as Mr. Hanson continued. "What's even stranger is that before I could respond, Jennifer and Anita jumped in to defend me and Andi stopped. The odd part is, these were the same kids who've been pretty hard to reach this fall. I'm not sure what happened?"

(Continued)

(Continued)

Ms. Harbez smiled knowingly. "Hanson, you're new here and none of the seniors know you and because this is their last year, they don't feel like they need to."

"Yeah, that about sums up these first few months I've been here," grumbled Mr. Hanson.

"So something has changed." Harbez stared at Hanson. "Are you involved in anything new?"

"Well, the student council asked me to volunteer as the teacher facilitator for the student council," he replied, still puzzled. "But what does that have to do with it?"

"Well," Ms. Harbez said, leaning in slightly, "Anita and a few of those students are involved in the student council, aren't they? So I would guess that your willingness to step up and support their interests outside of the classroom hasn't gone unnoticed. They're seeing you as more than just their math teacher. You're building a connection with them by showing you care about their activities and opinions."

Mr. Hanson nodded slowly as the realization sank in. "So, they're starting to respect me more because of that?"

"Exactly," Ms. Harbez affirmed. "It's not just about what happens in the classroom. Your actions outside of it can make a difference too."

"I have another question," Mr. Hanson said excitedly.

"What's that?" asked Ms. Harbez.

"What's Andi involved in?!?"

While building relationships is something that can neither be rushed or faked it can definitely be fostered through genuineness and patience. Steps can be taken to establish a conducive environment for getting to know your students. Here are some guiding ideas to assist you in fostering these relationships:

1. **Demonstrating Warmth.** Action truly does speak louder than words. Accepting your students for who they are, demonstrating genuine affection, practicing unconditional respect, and showing a positive regard for your students is vital to relationship building. Dr. Franita Ware's work on *Warm Demander Teachers*, inspires us to look at ourselves and embrace opportunities to demonstrate to all students in our classrooms (Ware, 2006, 2025).

2. **Establishing Trust.** When students see that their teacher believes in them, especially when they struggle, trust can be built. Teachers need to have the expectation that students will be successful and that what teachers want them to learn is

worth learning. Just remember, due to all types of harms and trauma, many of our students will take a longer time to come to trust you, thus you must lead by example over the long term.

3. **Employing Empathy.** Seeing the classroom and the various events and incidents that occur through the eyes of the students is important to entering into a relationship with the students. Teachers need to take the perspective of students if they are to reach them in a positive manner. When the teacher begins to truly understand the students in their care, they can tailor their own behavior, lessons, assessments, communication, and other interactions to their needs.

4. **Show Genuine Interest in Students' Lives.** Take the time to learn about your students' interests, hobbies, and backgrounds. Being open to conversations that go beyond academics, to their favorite teams, music or movie stars is an easy place to start. This shows students that you see them as individuals, not just learners in a classroom. When students feel that their teacher cares about them personally, they are more likely to feel connected and motivated to participate actively in class. A word of caution—you are not trying to become their friend thus personal topics or questions about more intimate topics should be avoided.

5. **Be Consistent and Fair.** Establish clear expectations and maintain consistency in how you apply rules and consequences. Fair treatment builds trust, as students need to know that they will be treated equally and with respect. When students can see their teacher as fair and dependable, they are more likely to respect authority and feel secure in the classroom environment. Consistency also includes following through on promises, whether it's providing feedback, recognizing achievements, or offering support when needed. It is important to remember that trust, like glass, is easily broken and very hard to repair.

6. **Encourage Open Communication.** Create a classroom atmosphere where students feel comfortable expressing their thoughts, concerns, and questions. This can be achieved by actively listening to students, providing opportunities for them to share their opinions, and responding thoughtfully to their input. Encourage feedback about your teaching methods and be open to making adjustments. When students feel heard, they are more likely to engage in learning and develop a stronger connection with their teacher. Remember to be clear if you are

asking for their input to explain if it will be used as guidance or the final word. Having students offer input and then for the other direction can be very disheartening for young people just as it is for adults.

As you engage in the relationship building process with your students it is imperative to remember that you as the teacher are always the one that must carry the olive branch. This means that we must understand there will be times when your students act a certain way (after all they are still kids) that you may not like but it is imperative they know you will always be there to support them. This is especially true when they act out, or make decisions that were not ideal. You are the teacher, and as such you have the responsibility to uphold these relationships. This isn't always easy, as there are times that students will test our patience but they need to know that you respect them, care about them, and truly want them to be successful.

QUESTIONS TO ASK YOUR MENTOR OR COLLEAGUES

1. How do you go about building relationships within your classroom at the start of the year and how do you maintain those relationships?
2. How do you repair relationships that have been damaged for one reason or another?

TOOLBOX TACTIC 5.6 CREATING A BRAVE SPACE

Case: *Brave spaces encourage open, honest conversations about identity and equity, recognizing that discomfort is essential for growth. They foster respect, vulnerability, and active listening, allowing participants to take risks, learn from mistakes, and engage in meaningful change.*

From Sarah: *Vulnerability can be daunting for students and teachers alike. Although I could never guarantee that my classroom was 100 percent safe at all times, I could ensure that for my students I would be honest, vulnerable, and brave for them, as an example to emulate. That didn't come overnight—it took time for me to realize the type of teacher I wanted to be.*

Often, we have heard that we want to make classrooms safe for all. While this is true, it is also impossible. Safety is not just the physical. Safety also refers to the psychological elements of a classroom. Being a trauma informed and culturally responsive teacher will support student growth and resilience by equipping them with the skills they may need to create that environment for themselves. This is especially important when navigating difficult conversations and tough topics with students. Having a conversation about racism, with a nearly entirely white class, for example, may not feel safe for the one racialized student in your classroom. There may be unnecessary attention drawn to that one student and, depending on how they navigate the conversation, they may not feel as though that is a safe place for them to be.

CULTIVATING BRAVE SPACES

How can teachers help to cocreate a brave space in the classroom with their students?

1. **Consider different perspectives.** Students will have different lived experiences based on where they come from, how they're raised, and the values they have. A student who is a refugee and new to the country will have a very different point of view than a student who was born and raised in the country you reside in.
2. **Define *brave*.** Allow students to explain what it means to be brave and describe or talk about a time when they had to be brave. An important step, as their teacher, is to take part in this exercise alongside them.
3. **Define *safe*.** In the same type of exercise, allow students to explain what it means to be safe and describe or talk about places where they feel safe. Again, take part in this exercise alongside them.
4. **Allow vulnerability.** When you don't know or understand something, model for students that it is okay to ask questions. Better yet, model for students the way to ask questions that won't offend. There are ways to ask questions appropriately and ways to offend with the questions you may have. Part of your job is to ensure that students know the difference.
5. **What are the intentions?** If students are looking to inquire about a topic, is the intention to put down or lift up?

By normalizing a brave space for students, you will see a shift in the culture of your classroom for the better. Students hearing one another in this space will reinforce how important it is to be resilient and brave and will give students the courage to be vulnerable in the space that you share.

QUESTIONS TO ASK YOUR MENTOR OR COLLEAGUES

1. What is the best way to reassure students that they are safe in school?
2. How can we encourage students to continue to stay brave?

BRINGING IT ALL TOGETHER

Never underestimate the impact your physical learning environment will have on the success of your students. Students who are learning in a place that is emotionally safe, academically rigorous, and culturally responsive, are more likely to flourish.

By now, you are most likely starting to realize that many of the presented toolbox tactics in this chapter are intrinsically related. The learning environment (while being one of the presented chapters), is critical to the successful implementation of other toolbox tactics and thus we feel it is important to communicate that we feel that you cannot have solid instructional and assessment practices (presented in the next few chapters) without an environment conducive for learning. Do not take this responsibility lightly, the environment and culture in which a student learns will equate to the degree of success of their growth and progress! Good luck with tracking your implementation of the learning environment, and do not underestimate the impact this will have on your teaching and the students' learning.

IMPLEMENTATION TRACKER

Attempted toolbox tactic:	
Successes:	Roadblocks:
What should I change to be more successful next time?	

Attempted toolbox tactic:	
Successes:	Roadblocks:
What should I change to be more successful next time?	

6

INSTRUCTIONAL PRACTICES: BUILDING A STRONG FOUNDATION IN THE CLASSROOM

Imagine stepping into your classroom for the first time, the room buzzing with potential, every desk waiting for a student, and the board ready for the first mark of the day. As a new teacher, it's exhilarating and maybe a little overwhelming. You've got your lesson plans, your materials, and a lot of enthusiasm—but what will truly make a difference in your students' learning experience is how you bring it all together through your instructional practices.

Instructional practices are the heartbeat of your teaching. They're the strategies, methods, and techniques you use to ensure that what you teach is understood, retained, and applied by your students. Effective instructional practices are not just about delivering content; they're about crafting an environment where learning can thrive. This means being intentional about how you communicate what students need to learn, how you engage them in thinking critically, and how you manage the classroom dynamics to create a space conducive to learning.

COMMUNICATING THE LEARNING: THE POWER OF CLARITY

One of the most crucial aspects of effective instruction is making sure that students know what they're expected to learn. This is where learning targets come in. Think of learning targets as the roadmap for your lesson. They are clear, concise statements that outline what students should know and be able to do by the end of a lesson or unit. When you start a lesson by sharing the learning target, you're setting the stage for purposeful learning. It's telling your students, "Here's where we're headed today, and this is why it matters." When students understand the goal, they're more likely to stay focused and engaged because they know what they're working toward. Plus, it gives them a sense of ownership over their learning—they can track their own progress and celebrate their successes.

ASKING THE RIGHT QUESTIONS: SPARKING CURIOSITY AND DEEP THINKING

Another cornerstone of effective instructional practice is the art of questioning. Good questions do more than just check for understanding; they ignite curiosity, provoke thought, and encourage students to explore ideas in depth. Effective questioning techniques involve asking open-ended questions that challenge students to think critically and express their reasoning. Instead of asking, "Did you understand the lesson?" you might ask, "How does this concept connect to what we learned yesterday?" or "What evidence can you find to support your answer?" These kinds of questions prompt students to make connections, analyze information, and articulate their understanding in a way that deepens their learning.

CLASSROOM MANAGEMENT: CREATING A POSITIVE LEARNING ENVIRONMENT

Of course, even the best instructional practices can fall flat without strong classroom management. This doesn't mean being strict or controlling—it's about creating a learning environment that is orderly, respectful, and supportive. Classroom management is the backbone that allows your instructional strategies to flourish. A well-managed classroom is one where students feel safe to take risks, share their ideas, and make mistakes. It's a space where routines are established, expectations are clear, and students know what is expected of them. When students feel that they are in a structured environment, they're more likely to engage with the material and participate actively in their learning.

STUDENT ENGAGEMENT: THE HEART OF EFFECTIVE INSTRUCTION

At the end of the day, all the strategies in the world won't matter if students aren't engaged. Engagement is what turns passive listening into active learning. It's about creating lessons that captivate students' interests, connect with their experiences, and challenge them to think deeply. Engaging students means varying your instructional methods—mixing direct instruction with collaborative learning, integrating technology, and incorporating hands-on activities. It's also about building relationships and getting to know your students as individuals, so you can tailor your instruction to their needs and interests. When students are engaged, they're not just learning—they're invested in their learning.

THE PATH TO EFFECTIVE TEACHING

Solid instructional practices are the foundation of effective teaching. By clearly communicating learning goals, asking thoughtful questions, managing your classroom well, and keeping students engaged, you're setting the stage for meaningful learning. Remember, great teaching isn't about being perfect; it's about being purposeful. With these practices in your toolkit, you'll be well on your way to creating a classroom environment where both you and your students can thrive.

As you embark through the rest of this chapter, we wanted to make sure you had a clear map of the concepts and ideas that will be explored more in depth. As we mentioned previously in the introduction, do not feel pressured to try and apply all of these ideas; rather explore as many of these as you can and apply what piques your interests or needs. Enjoy exploring the following toolbox tactics:

1. Classroom Management: A big driver for student engagement is how we manage our learning environment. Looking beyond student behavior will help us understand how best to manage our class.

2. Restorative Justice: Looking at using dialogue and conversation to mitigate future class flare ups is the fundamental reason for restorative justice and restorative practices. When we open a dialogue with students, we can get a greater understanding of why our students may be acting the way they do.
3. The Importance of Communicating Learning to Students: Students are more likely to engage in the learning process when they are aware and are able to iterate the reasons why they are learning what they are learning, and what successful learning looks like in a classroom context.
4. Learner Engagement: Our students come to us with a variety of engagement levels. Knowing how to navigate through a lesson to promote different levels of engagement will help the impact of your teaching.
5. Developing Your Questioning Techniques: It is important for us to move beyond surface level questioning, toward questions that grab student's interests and require them to do the heavy lifting of the learning.

TOOLBOX TACTIC 6.1 CLASSROOM MANAGEMENT

Case: *Effective classroom management is crucial for new teachers because it forms the foundation for a productive learning environment. Without solid management practices, even the most well-planned lessons can fall apart due to disruptions or a lack of focus. A rich understanding of classroom management strategies will enable you to create a structured and supportive environment where students feel safe, respected, and motivated to learn. We will guide you through some of the main reasons why a student might not be exhibiting appropriate behaviours and provide some guidance on how to help you get them to engage in their learning more positively.*

From Vince: *There were days after teaching my eighth-grade class where I was exhausted, the students and I were not on the same wavelength, and it seemed like everything I would try would be met with resistance and off task behavior. I had issues with my management skills and needed help. After talking with a colleague of mine, they suggested I look at external aspects of my lesson and not place direct and exclusive blame on the students. What was I doing to manage or promote off task behavior? This conversation dramatically changed my approach to classroom management.*

LOOK BEYOND THE BEHAVIOR

Fact: Students will make poor choices on occasion, and this will likely prove to be a source of frustration for you. Let's explore how to decrease your frustration and build confidence in your repertoire of classroom management techniques. We have talked about the importance of relationships, knowing your learners (the "who" before we "do"), leveraging your classroom environment as the third teacher, and how to use great questions to engage students. Yet, sometimes your student is still not listening, is disruptive, exhibits violent outbursts, or is lethargic and completely disengaged. What is a new teacher to do?

In this section, we begin by sharing some of the main reasons why students make poor choices, are dysregulated and exhibit behaviors contrary to what is expected for successful learning. We want to equip you with a frame of reference that, as difficult as it may seem, seeks to help you to see the student separately from the behaviour. So, before any logical consequences are applied or disciplinary actions taken, try to see the human being first and the poor behaviour second. To better understand the causes of poor or unexpected behaviour, let's start with a quick examination of the word *dysregulation*.

Dysregulated refers to the inability to regulate emotions, behaviors, or physiological processes effectively. It's often used in psychological and medical contexts to describe someone who has difficulty managing emotional responses or maintaining stable internal states. For example, someone might be described as having "emotional dysregulation" if they frequently experience intense emotions that are difficult to control. If we want our students to be better at self-regulation, it is helpful to consider the sources of the student behaviors.

STUDENT MISBEHAVIOR

Here are some of the most common reasons why students might misbehave:

Lack of engagement: When lessons are not engaging or fail to capture students' interest, they may become bored and act out to entertain themselves or gain attention.

Unclear expectations: If students are unsure about what is expected of them regarding behavior and academic performance, they may inadvertently misbehave due to confusion or frustration.

Seeking attention: Some students misbehave to gain attention from their peers or the teacher, especially if they feel neglected or overlooked in a large class.

Frustration with difficulty: When students find the material too difficult or overwhelming, they may act out in frustration or to avoid tasks they find challenging.

Lack of routine and structure: Inconsistent routines or a lack of structure can make students feel insecure and uncertain, leading to disruptive behavior as they test boundaries or seek control.

Peer influence: Students may misbehave to fit in with or impress their peers, especially if they are part of a group that values disruptive behavior.

Emotional or personal issues: Personal problems, such as family issues, stress, or emotional difficulties, can cause students to misbehave as a way to express their feelings or cope with their situation.

Desire for power and control: Some students may misbehave to assert control or challenge authority, particularly if they feel powerless in other areas of their lives.

Unmet social-emotional needs: Students who lack social-emotional skills, such as empathy or self-regulation, may struggle to manage their behavior in a classroom setting.

Learning or behavioral disorders: Some students may have underlying learning or behavioral disorders, such as ADHD or autism, that contribute to disruptive behavior in class.

Understanding these reasons can help new teachers develop targeted strategies to address the underlying causes of misbehavior and create a more positive learning environment. Notice that the first six reasons wherein problems might occur, are largely under the direct control of you, the teacher. Your lesson design, classroom set-up, routines, seating plans and communication protocols go a long way to being proactive and preventing unexpected behaviours before they start. The last items on the list, however, take us into the socioemotional realities (which include trauma) and the special education needs that a child might present.

Looking beyond the unexpected or disruptive behavior and seeing the student first is what we have emphasized is key to successfully addressing the undesired behavior. What we want to do now is give you some tools that are known to be helpful in helping students self-regulate and we know that effective classroom management is key to creating a positive learning environment. Here are some strategies and techniques that can help you as a new teacher:

1. **Create Engaging Lessons**
   - Variety in Teaching Methods: Use a mix of teaching strategies to cater to different learning styles (e.g., group work, discussions, games, questions, hands-on activities).
   - Pacing: Keep lessons moving at a pace that maintains student interest and minimizes downtime, which can lead to disruptions. Be sure to factor in movement breaks.
2. **Establish Clear Expectations**
   - Set Rules Early: Clearly define classroom rules and expectations from day one. Make sure they are simple, specific, and achievable. Include students in the setting of rules if possible.
   - Consistency: Be consistent in enforcing rules and procedures. Inconsistency can lead to confusion and challenges. Talk to your admin and grade partners to maximize consistency throughout the school.
3. **Build Relationships**
   - Get to Know Your Students: Learn their names, interests, and backgrounds. Building rapport helps in gaining respect and understanding their needs.
   - Positive Reinforcement: Acknowledge good behavior and achievements, which encourages students to continue those behaviors. A note or card, a positive call or email to a parent can go a long way.
4. **Classroom Layout**
   - Seating Arrangements: Arrange desks to facilitate learning and minimize distractions. You can experiment with different setups (e.g., rows, clusters, U-shape).
   - Movement: Position yourself strategically in the classroom to monitor students and engage with them. Use your proximity and move to potential hot spots before they flare up.

5. **Proactive Classroom Routines**
   - Routine and Procedures: Establish routines for common tasks (e.g., turning in assignments, starting class) so students know what to expect.
   - Anticipate Issues: Recognize potential problems before they escalate. For example, if a student looks disengaged, redirect their attention before they become disruptive.
6. **Effective Communication**
   - Clear Instructions: Give clear, concise instructions and check for understanding. Avoid vague directions that could lead to confusion. Learning intentions and success criteria are essential.
   - Nonverbal Cues: Use eye contact, hand signals, or proximity to communicate and manage behavior subtly.
7. **Reflect and Adjust**
   - Reflect on Lessons: After each class, reflect on what worked and what didn't. Adjust your strategies as needed.
   - Seek Feedback: Don't hesitate to ask colleagues or even students for feedback on your classroom management.
8. **Stay Calm and Patient**
   - Manage Your Emotions: Stay calm in the face of challenges. Your composure sets the tone for the classroom.
   - Patience: Give students time to adjust to your expectations, especially if they are different from what they are used to.
9. **Utilize Technology Wisely**
   - Interactive Tools: Incorporate technology like smartboards, educational apps, or online resources to make lessons more engaging and organized.
   - Monitor Usage: Ensure that students are using technology appropriately and not as a distraction.
10. **Professional Development**
    - Continuous Learning: Attend workshops, read books, and engage in professional development focused on classroom management.

By implementing these strategies, you'll create a structured, supportive environment where students can thrive.

SCHOOL STORIES

The State of Pat's Grade 8

Pat, a first-year teacher, was experiencing some challenging behaviors from Grade 8 students. The students were full of energy, constantly chatting, fidgeting, and paying little attention to Pat's instructions. Despite best efforts, Pat struggled to maintain order in the classroom. Each day seemed to end with Pat feeling more frustrated and defeated.

One afternoon, after a particularly chaotic class, Pat decided to seek advice from a mentor teacher, Ms. Harper. Ms. Harper had been teaching at River Valley Community School for over 20 years and was known for her engaging lessons and well-managed classroom. She welcomed Pat into her cozy, plant-filled classroom, offering a warm smile as Pat sank into a wicker chair.

"I'm trying everything, but the kids just won't listen," Pat confessed, the frustration evident in a wavering voice. "They talk over me, they're distracted, and I can't seem to keep them focused."

Ms. Harper nodded thoughtfully. "It's tough when you're starting out, but don't worry—it gets better. Let's talk about some strategies that can help. Have you tried prompting and cueing?"

Pat frowned slightly. "I've given them reminders, but it doesn't seem to work."

"Prompting and cueing go beyond just reminders," Ms. Harper explained. "It's about setting clear expectations before transitions or activities. For example, before starting a new lesson, give them a heads-up about what you expect—like, 'In two minutes, I want everyone to have their books out and be ready to listen.' Then use a consistent cue, like raising your hand or dimming the lights, to signal when it's time to be quiet."

Pat nodded, taking mental notes. "That makes sense. I haven't really thought about how I'm cueing them."

Ms. Harper leaned in, her tone gentle but firm. "Another thing that can make a big difference is your proximity. Instead of addressing the whole class from the front, try walking around the room. Stand near the students who are off task or chatty. Often, just your presence will remind them to stay on track."

"I usually stay by the whiteboard when I'm teaching," Pat admitted. "I guess I could move around more."

"Exactly," Ms. Harper encouraged. "And don't underestimate the power of communication protocols. Teach them how to respond to your

(Continued)

(Continued)

cues—like raising their hands or responding with a specific word when you ask for their attention. It might take some practice, but once they get used to it, you'll find it easier to get their focus."

Pat felt a flicker of hope. "I hadn't thought about it that way. I'll give it a try."

Ms. Harper smiled warmly. "Remember, it's a process. Be consistent, and don't be afraid to reinforce these strategies. With time, you'll see improvement."

Pat left Ms. Harper's classroom with a renewed sense of determination. The next day, armed with new strategies and a fresh perspective, Pat began to implement the advice. It wasn't a miracle cure, but slowly, positive change become noticeable. The students responded more readily to cues, paid closer attention, and the classroom became a bit more orderly.

Pat knew there was still a long way to go, but for the first time, felt increasing levels of confidence and support knowing that great mentor teachers, like Ms. Harper, were available to offer a helping hand.

COFFEE TALK WITH PAT

Imagine that you are Pat's colleague and over coffee, Pat recounts the struggles with the Grade 8 class to you. What advice, actions, or ideas from this *Toolbox Tactic* would you suggest Pat also consider? Add your ideas in the space provided.

QUESTIONS TO ASK YOUR MENTOR OR COLLEAGUES

1. How can I effectively establish and enforce classroom rules and expectations without seeming too strict?
2. What are some strategies to engage students who seem disinterested or disruptive?
3. How can I maintain consistency in my classroom management while still being flexible to individual student needs?
4. What are some nonverbal cues or techniques I can use to manage behavior discreetly?
5. How should I reflect on and adjust my classroom management strategies throughout the school year?

TOOLBOX TACTIC 6.2 RESTORATIVE JUSTICE MODEL

Case: *All people seek relationships and connections with others. We require many things in order to feel whole, but one of the things that is most important is positive relationships with those around us. The restorative justice model is meant to mend relationships that may have been severed by actions, language, or intentions.*

From Sarah: *One of the best ways to repair relationships is to dialogue. Restorative justice focuses on repairing harm through accountability, conversation, and understanding. It helps build relationships, fosters respect, and teaches conflict resolution, creating a more inclusive and supportive environment. Learning from Indigenous Elders and Knowledge Keepers about this practice was a highlight for me as a consultant. In fact, the skills learned are skills that I have used in my everyday life!*

WHAT IS THE RESTORATIVE JUSTICE MODEL?

The restorative justice model studies how to strengthen relationships between individuals as well as social connections within communities. These practices have deep roots within global Indigenous communities. It is meant to mend relationships without punitive actions. Difficult conversations are had amongst all parties—those who were harmed and those who caused harm, as well as their support systems. Restorative justice is meant to encourage dialogue to bring people back together in an effort to keep relationships whole. A restorative conference can range from two people and can be upward of 15; this is dependent on how many people are involved in the conflict. A restorative conference can range from an informal conversation to a full conference with mediation.

It is important to note that, most of the time, people want to do the right thing. Most of the time, people do not want to cause harm. In the event that harm is caused, especially in a school setting, we can look to restoring the relationship rather than suspension or expulsion. Restorative practices enable the rejection of unacceptable behavior due to unmet expectations or standards, while still recognizing the inherent value of the individual and their potential positive impact on society.

THE PRINCIPLES OF RESTORATIVE JUSTICE

1. **Repairing Harm**: The main goal is to address and repair the harm caused. This involves acknowledging the impact on those who are harmed, those who caused harm, and the community at large.
2. **Accountability**: Those who caused harm are encouraged, through this process, to take responsibility and see the negative impact of the actions taken.
3. **Inclusion**: In the process of restoring and mending a relationship, everyone has the opportunity to speak their truth and have a voice. Collectively, a solution is created and everyone's point of view is heard.
4. **Transformation**: This process is meant to transform all of the parties involved. It allows everyone to listen and learn from the point of view of all parties involved. The hope is that there is positive change that will come from a restorative conference.

Restorative justice is successful because it focuses on healing rather than punishment. By prioritizing the repair of harm caused by criminal behavior, it addresses the needs of victims, offenders, and the community. This approach fosters accountability, as offenders are encouraged to take responsibility for their actions and make amends. The inclusive nature of restorative justice allows all stakeholders to participate in the process, promoting understanding and empathy.

Additionally, it strengthens community bonds and helps prevent future offenses by addressing the root causes of criminal behavior. Overall, Restorative justice creates a more compassionate and effective justice system that benefits everyone involved.

QUESTIONS FOR YOUR MENTOR OR COLLEAGUES

1. What methods does our school use when harm is caused?
2. Is this a realistic method to support our students?
3. How can we make restorative conferences work for our school community?

TOOLBOX TACTIC 6.3 THE IMPORTANCE OF COMMUNICATING LEARNING TO STUDENTS

Case: *Picture this, you are taking on a new teaching position that involves teaching a course (or multiple courses) that you have never taught before. Determining the path to teach can be daunting, but what is more daunting is communicating this path to your students. Incorporating aspects of clarity of communication is essential to ensure your students are aware of their learning and are not simply on a "need to know"; basis.*

From Vince: *For me personally, when I know more about a task I am about to engage with I am more likely to really put forth an effort to get the job done. It helps me to know what the end result looks like, and allows me to better conceptualize a path to accomplishment. This is the same for many of our students, in communicating the forward path of learning they are much more likely to engage in behaviors that further complement their learning.*

Earlier in this book, we spent time discussing the importance of planning and knowing the program you are delivering to ensure you construct a proper path to mastery for your students (Toolbox Tactics 3.1 and 3.2). Once you have a grasp of this, the next logical step is to ensure you are communicating the learning to your students. When established as a proper routine or procedure, implementing aspects of clarity throughout your instruction will support the learning process your students are embarking upon.

WHAT IS CLARITY IN THE CLASSROOM?

Before jumping into talking about incorporating aspects of clarity in your instructional practice, it is important to talk about what it is. Often when I (Vince) am doing workshops that include aspects of clarity, I find there are multiple interpretations of what it is versus what it is not. Firstly though, it is important for us to recognize the brilliant work that has been done in the space of teacher clarity by some of our friends in the academic space. There are playbooks on teacher clarity, and other research conducted in the *Visible Learning* space that complement and enhance the messages presented in this toolbox tactic, and should you want to explore these further we will add the titles at the end of this chapter for you to search on your own. For the purpose of this tactic, we will explore the principles of clarity as described by Fendick's (1990) meta-analysis. The study summarized the pillars or principles of clarity as follows:

- *Clarity of Organization*: This can be summarized by considering the way teachers organize their lessons, and the impact of using our standards to drive our planning process. The order in which these are delivered to students should build toward mastery of these objectives.
- *Clarity of Explanation*: This is summarized by considering the way we communicate the learning to our students. There is a delicate balance between using student friendly language but also still honoring the academic language and vocabulary students should know.
- *Clarity of Examples and Guided Practice*: This principle considers the extent to which we provide students with success criteria, exemplars, or examples in which they can use to identify what success looks like in learning.
- *Clarity in Assessments:* This can be summarized (and will be discussed more in the next chapter) as the steps teachers take to incorporate student voice into assessments, as well as using assessments to inform their own practice. This also factors in the extent to which teachers are using a feedback loop and incorporating student feedback on their own practice.

Each of these pillars are significant in their own right, yet for the sake of this tactic we will use the messages from these pillars to discuss how to make this work in our classrooms.

COMMUNICATING THE PATH FOR STUDENTS

Communicating the learning path to students is critical to the incorporation of clarity in the classroom, and the focus of our communication should specifically focus on the concepts in which students are learning, and the skills and processes needed to demonstrate they have met their learning. Fisher et al. (2016) refer to three specific questions students should be able to answer as they engage with your lessons. Those questions are (1) What am I learning today? (2) Why am I learning this? and (3) How will I know I have learned it? Let's look at what each of these mean a bit more in depth.

WHAT AM I LEARNING TODAY?

As students engage with the lesson they deserve to know what they are learning about. It is our responsibility to craft statements that describe the concepts and contexts of what our students are learning. These are commonly referred to as learning intentions in the *Visible Learning* research, but have been known to be called learning targets, or learning objectives. It is possible that your school or district may have something like this embedded in practice already! Nonetheless, the goal here is for us to begin a class with the daily or weekly intention of what we want our students to learn. These intentions are often crafted using the concepts and contexts from our standards.

WHY AM I LEARNING THIS?

Often coconstructed with students, we can provide reasoning as to why our learning intention (objective, target, etc.) is significant to our students. This can be a rationale that is important to the students' life or to their academic progress. The goal here is to have a conversation with the class about the relevance of their learning and through this conversation, students can make connections to the purpose of learning.

HOW WILL I KNOW I HAVE LEARNED IT?

Perhaps the most important question our students should be able to answer, this factors in the indicators of success or progress that students should exemplify as they move through their learning. In the *Visible Learning* research and across other academic research these statements are often called success criteria. For this to operate effectively in our classrooms, we should create statements that unpack the verbs in the standard and craft them in a manner that increases in complexity. These are generally manifested as *I can* statements and use the verbs presented to us in our standards. To clarify the layout of these statements paired with a learning intention, we have included an example later in this tactic.

It is important as we help clarify the path to learning for our students that we communicate the learning as an iterative process that is more about the journey than the destination. Meaning that learning occurs despite of products students create and reflecting upon the learning specifically will improve growth and achievement. This can be done by keeping the following two concepts as the main message behind the journey to answering the three questions. Firstly, we must communicate and ensure students understand that the learning target or learning intention is the end point of the learning (or the off ramp of learning). What we mean by this is that when we present the answer to the question "What am I learning today?" to our students, we impart the understanding they should not be expected to know that yet. This makes more sense when we consider the second concept which is that in order to meet the answer to the first question we must understand that the success criteria provides checkpoints to understanding. Thus, as we meet each checkpoint we get closer and closer to achieving the learning intention.

SUPPORTING YOUR DELIVERY

As you begin to hone your clarity messages in your classroom we wanted to provide you with a few sentence frames for your learning

6.1 Supportive Sentence Frames

Learning Intention: **Structure:** We are learning about (<u>**CONCEPT**</u>) + (<u>**CONTEXT**</u>). **Example:** We are learning about the <u>**balance of powers**</u> among the <u>**three branches of government**</u>.
Success Criteria: **Structure: I can (<u>VERB</u>) . . .** **Examples:** • I can <u>**name**</u> the three branches of government. • I can <u>**describe**</u> the function of each branch of government. • I can <u>**compare**</u> the roles of each branch of government.

intentions and success criteria. Please remember there are multiple ways to present the information to your students as you prepare them to answer the three questions, however the example shown in Figure 6.1 is a great place to start. Give these sentence frames a try as you communicate the learning to our students.

QUESTIONS TO ASK YOUR MENTOR OR COLLEAGUES

1. Does our school or district implement aspects of teacher clarity, and if so do they have resources or tools to support?
2. How do you communicate the learning to your students to ensure they are able to answer the questions?
3. How might you use exemplars, examples, or other artifacts to help students understand what success looks like?

TOOLBOX TACTIC 6.4 LEARNER ENGAGEMENT

Case: *Looking out across classrooms, it is clear that our understanding of student engagement has changed. No more can teachers simply command attention and engagement. It is vital we understand we need to earn engagement by preceding well-crafted and thought-out materials. And while more and more districts and jurisdictions are regulating or straight up banning personal devices at least in classrooms, teachers must seize the moment to reengage learners now while the opportunity exists. How do you intend on engaging your learners?*

From Tim: *In my early years of teaching, I relied on humour, storytelling and inviting students to share their experiences to engage them in the learning outcomes. Now, there are so many competing influences trying to win our attention. Increased use of technology and our decreasing levels of working memory make it harder to focus and engage with the task at hand. To teach, we must reach our learners. Engaging them in their learning is key to reducing boredom and empowering them to be active participants in their learning experiences. Humour, stories, and student voice and choice in learning are more important now than ever.*

RULES OF ENGAGEMENT

Picture in your mind a large staircase like the ones outside museums and town halls bustling with people moving up and down the steps, a flurry of motion. These stairs are a metaphor for student engagement in the classroom. Each step represents increasing (or decreasing) involvement, enthusiasm, and commitment for learning. This movement up and down the stairs represents their engagement with their education, continually influenced by a variety of factors—many being within your control. Let's also be clear that these steps do not, at least for this moment represent achievement, just levels of engagement.

Across these steps (see Figure 6.2) students range in their engagement in the lessons in front of them. Those at the highest step are actively participating in class discussions, eagerly completing assignments while others may be moving closer or farther away from that level. As Berry (2020, 2023) posits, students are not just engaged or disengaged and in fact can move across a continuum of levels of engagement. Think of how you engaged with your college courses and when you were most "into it" and other times when you suddenly realized the professor was talking and you had missed the last few minutes thinking of what you would be making for dinner that night.

6.2 Steps to Student Engagement

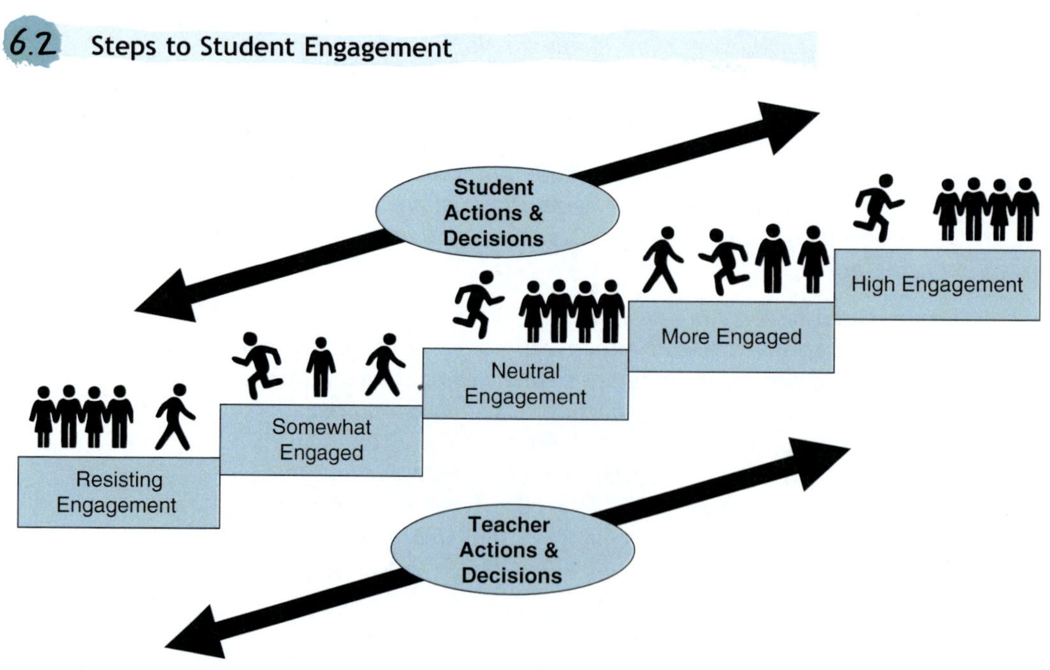

Icon Sources: istock.com/aelitta; istock.com/bubaone

The students standing on that top step are driven by a genuine interest in the subject matter and a desire to excel. Students such as these often set the tone for the classroom, encouraging others to climb higher by modeling positive behaviors and attitudes. Teachers can help these students by providing them with challenges that stimulate their curiosity, offering opportunities for leadership, and recognizing their efforts with feedback.

However, students' engagement can wane, causing them to travel down the stairs. Students who are a few steps down are still involved but perhaps not as consistently or enthusiastically as their peers farther above. They might contribute to discussions but will not take the lead, or they might complete assignments but just do the minimum required. These students must be encouraged to climb back up and not continue their downward slide.

Teachers play a pivotal role in these moments by identifying the factors contributing to this disengagement. Whether it's a lack of understanding, external pressures, or a need for more support specific help is needed in the form of targeted interventions. Understanding that you as the professional can have a determining effect on their engagement level is key to both of your success. These interventions might include offering additional help, adjusting teaching methods to better align with the student's learning style, or simply showing a genuine interest in their well-being.

As students continue down the stairs, their disengagement manifests more clearly. They might show up to class physically but not mentally, daydreaming instead of participating, turning in work that lacks effort and thought. These students are on the brink of complete disengagement, and your role as the teacher becomes even more crucial. Your actions can inadvertently push these students further down the stairs by failing to address their needs or using punitive measures instead of support. For instance, if a student is struggling with a concept and you do not notice or provide the right help, that student might become frustrated, lose confidence, and disengage further.

At the bottom of the stairs are the fully disengaged or even disruptive. These learners have lost interest in their education, often skipping classes, not completing assignments, feeling disconnected from the school and its environment. For these students, the educational experience has become a source of stress rather than excitement or growth. Teachers can help these students begin the climb back up by creating a supportive and inclusive classroom environment, reaching out to understand the root causes of their disengagement, and implementing personalized strategies to reengage them. This might include differentiating instruction to make learning more accessible, fostering a sense of community within the classroom, or connecting the curriculum to the student's interests and goals.

It is vitally important that you do your utmost to remain objective in these moments, searching for clues to explain what is going on. Becoming emotionally invested to the point you are "riding the roller coaster" with the student is unwise as you will miss important clues. A great hockey player once said that if he, as captain, could understand the motivating factors of his teammates he could lead them much more easily than by shouting empty clichés about "giving it your all" or "It's go time." Some students who struggle would rather "fail cool" than look like a failure and thus will suddenly withdraw from the learning environment than let you see their true struggles with literacy or numeracy or the traumas that have shaped them.

Ultimately, the journey up and down the stairs of engagement is anything but static as students, for a variety of personal and school reasons, find themselves on a number of steps during the school day or that matter, the same class. Please remember, you hold a significant influence over whether students ascend or descend these steps. By recognizing where each student is and responding with empathy, support, and appropriate challenges, teachers can help guide their students upward, fostering a more engaged and motivated learning environment.

DO NOT FORGET THE LESSON OF THE THREE BEARS

Student boredom is a killer for engagement. Avoiding student boredom is crucial for maintaining engagement and promoting effective learning. One of the most effective ways teachers can do this is by using formative assessment to determine the most appropriate starting point in a unit of study. Formative assessments, such as quizzes, discussions, or quick polls, allow teachers to gauge students' prior knowledge, skills, and understanding before diving into new material.

By assessing where students currently stand, teachers can tailor their instruction to meet students where they are, avoiding the risk of covering material that is too easy or too challenging. If a lesson begins with concepts students already know well, they may quickly lose interest and disengage. Conversely, if the material is too advanced, students may become frustrated or overwhelmed, leading to a similar loss of engagement.

Starting at the right level ensures that students are appropriately challenged, which keeps them actively involved and motivated. This approach not only prevents boredom but also fosters a more inclusive and supportive learning environment, where each student feels that their needs are being met. In this way, formative assessment is a powerful tool for enhancing student engagement and success throughout a unit of study.

STRATEGY

Engaging students in a new unit of study before it begins can set the tone for a successful and dynamic learning experience. One effective strategy is to spark curiosity and connect the upcoming material to students' interests and real-world applications. Here's how you can do this:

1. *Preview With a Provocative Question or Scenario*: Start by posing an intriguing question or presenting a real-life scenario related to the new unit that encourages students to think critically. For example, if the unit is on environmental science, you might ask, "What would happen if all the bees in the world disappeared?" This not only grabs attention but also invites students to start thinking about the topic before formal instruction begins.

2. *Use Engaging Media*: Show a short video clip, play a podcast, or share an article that highlights an interesting aspect of the unit. Media that tells a compelling story or presents surprising facts can captivate students and make them eager to learn more.

3. *Incorporate a Hands-On or Interactive Activity*: Before introducing the unit, engage students with an activity that relates to the content. For instance, in a unit on physics, you could have students participate in a simple experiment that demonstrates a principle they'll explore in depth later. This hands-on approach builds excitement and makes abstract concepts more tangible.

4. *Create a Connection to Students' Lives*: Relate the new unit to students' personal experiences, current events, or popular culture. By showing how the content is relevant to their world,

you help students see the value in what they're about to learn, which can increase their motivation and engagement.

5. *Encourage Pre-Unit Exploration:* Assign a brief research task or project that encourages students to explore the topic on their own before the unit begins. This could be as simple as finding one interesting fact or example related to the topic. When students come back to class, they can share what they discovered, creating a sense of ownership and curiosity about the new unit.

By using these strategies, you can effectively engage students before a new unit even begins, laying a strong foundation for active learning and deeper exploration of the subject matter.

QUESTIONS TO ASK YOUR MENTOR OR COLLEAGUES

1. What are some practices you use when you feel engagement slipping during a lesson?
2. How do you find an appropriate starting place if the room is "all over the place" according to formative assessment?

TOOLBOX TACTIC 6.5 DEVELOPING YOUR QUESTIONING TECHNIQUES (THE ART OF QUESTIONING)

Case: *As a new teacher, using effective questioning techniques can greatly enhance student engagement and learning. What are some questioning techniques known to have a high impact on student learning? To what extent are you able to engage students in formulating and asking questions that will aid them in their learning? As teachers, we know that the art of knowing how to ask good questions can have a large impact on guiding student learning. Knowing a variety of effective inquiry techniques will help you to increase student engagement, reinforce key learning concepts, and get valuable feedback on how well your students are understanding their learning tasks.*

From Wayne: *Learning when, how, and what to ask questions will save you a great deal of time and work as a teacher. Formative assessment can take many forms and all of them can lead you to discoveries that are important to your teaching. Once I learned this lesson as a young teacher,*

> *I become much better at knowing where to start with my students which helped me avoid boring or overwhelming them as learners. I also learned what interested them and I discovered many things about the communities that I taught in, that I would have not learned otherwise.*

MOVING BEYOND BASIC QUESTIONING

The who-what-when-where-why-how approach (W5+H), is most likely the way you were taught to gather information. These classic question stems are helpful for finding facts and getting key information but often do not go beyond a surface level of knowing or understanding. While the W5+H suite of questions is still important and useful, you will want to have some different tools that will help you to unlock deeper levels of inquiry and knowledge transfer for your students. We will explore a variety of techniques for you to consider and try with your students. Let's think of this as "the art of questioning."

Here are some well-known approaches that teachers use in questioning:

Open-Ended vs. Closed-Ended	Open-ended questions allow for multiple perspectives and deeper thinking, while close-ended questions typically have a single correct answer and are useful for checking basic understanding. For example, instead of asking, *"Did you like the story?"* you could ask, *"What did you think about the main character's decision?"*
Wait Time	After asking a question, give students time to think before they answer. This can lead to more thoughtful and complete responses. Feel comfortable giving several seconds of wait time (don't rush to an answer).
Probing Questions	Follow up on students' answers with questions that prompt them to expand or clarify their thoughts. For example, *"Can you explain why you think that?"* or *"What evidence supports your answer?"*

(Continued)

(Continued)

Higher-Order vs. Lower-Order Questions	Lower-order questions (e.g., recall and comprehension) check basic understanding, while higher-order questions (e.g., analysis, synthesis, evaluation) encourage deeper cognitive processing. Structure questions around Bloom's taxonomy to target different cognitive levels, from simple recall of facts *("What is the capital of France?")* to higher-order thinking like analysis and evaluation *("Why do you think the French Revolution happened?")*.
Formative Feedback and Follow-Up	Provide constructive feedback to student answers, and ask follow-up questions to probe deeper into their reasoning. This helps students refine their thinking and articulate their ideas more clearly. Use student responses to inform your teaching. Adjust your lesson plans and strategies based on the feedback you receive from questioning.
Inclusive Questioning	Students should feel comfortable asking and answering questions without fear of judgment. This encourages active participation and a positive learning atmosphere. Techniques like cold calling (randomly selecting students to answer) or think-pair-share (where students first think individually, then discuss with a partner before sharing with the class) can help involve everyone in the learning.
No Opt-Out	Acknowledge effort even when answers are incorrect. Acknowledge the student's effort and guide them toward the correct understanding. If a student

No Opt-Out (Continued)	doesn't know the answer, provide hints or ask another student, but then return to the original student to allow them to answer. This ensures everyone is involved and learning.
Funnel Questions	Start with broad questions and narrow down to more specific ones. This helps students focus their thinking and delve deeper into the topic. *"What are important forms of transportation." "How might bus service be improved in our town?" How efficient are propane powered school busses compared to diesel?*
Checking for Understanding	Regularly ask questions to gauge whether students are following along. Use questions like *"Who would like to summarize what we've just learned?"* or *"Does anyone have any questions about this?"*
Differentiated Questions	Tailor your questions to the varied skill levels in your classroom. Ask more challenging questions to advanced students and simpler ones to those who might be struggling, ensuring everyone is engaged at their level.
Reflective Questions	Encourage students to reflect on their learning process and how they arrived at an answer. Questions like *"How did you come to that conclusion?"* help students internalize their thinking process.

Incorporating these techniques can help you foster a dynamic and inclusive classroom environment where all students feel valued and challenged.

HAVE FUN USING QUESTIONS

Effective questioning techniques can go a long way in terms of classroom management. By keeping students engaged through inquiry, curiosity and wonder (the power of great questions), you will be able to gain greater levels of learner feedback and be able to determine who understands well and who might need some more support. Here are a few fun techniques that I (Tim) devised over the years and have enjoyed using in class.

- **Live Auction**—Ask a question: for example, "Who can tell me one important aspect of photosynthesis?" Pause for two seconds and then go into auctioneer mode. Ask "Who wishes to answer? Raise your hand." As hands go up, simply count them out loud: " I see one hand; do I have two? I have two hands; is there a third? Oh, I see four. Can I have five? I see five hands; how about six?" Essentially, try to get as many hands as possible and then pick a student to respond. This gives you a quick check as to which students feel confident to respond. Students like the fun of the fast pace counting of hands.
- **Echo**—As soon as a student answers a question correctly, I go to three or four students around the room and simply ask them to repeat (echo) what was said. This reinforces the concept (not just correct answer) and allows students who normally might not raise their hand (as in the auction technique) to repeat a correct answer. This is a low-stakes way to encourage the participation of reluctant students and also keeps all students on their toes for listening to their peers. By offering praise—a simple thank you—as you move on to the next student to echo the same answer, you increase motivation and impart a sense of participation in the reluctant student.
- **Point and Counterpoint**—I enjoy using this approach, especially in secondary classes. Raise an open-ended or debate style question and invite two students to share their response. One student must argue in favor, the other against. In each case, facts and conceptual considerations are applied. Then invite other students to share a comment (with evidence or rationale) in support of the argument (point) or against the argument (counterpoint). Encourage as many students as possible to participate so as to explore or exhaust all possible aspects of the argument. Think of this as a mini-debate.
- **Radio Call in Game Show**—This is a good technique for lesson review and for cold calling on reluctant students. Pretend you are

the on-air personality, and you are phoning listeners. Use local town names and neighborhood names to connect to the student. "Okay, we are going live out to Parksville this afternoon and I have (student name) on the line." Invite the student to answer. If stuck, they can call a friend. Once an answer is given, I go to the echo technique to reinforce the correct answer.

Again, the intention here is to show you some examples of fun ways to use questions to review key learning outcomes and keep students engaged. Our challenge to you is to try the sample techniques we have shared and to come up with some questioning approaches of your own. Encourage your students to create questioning games too.

QUESTIONS TO ASK YOUR MENTOR OR COLLEAGUES

As a new teacher, asking the right questions to a mentor can provide valuable insights into effective questioning techniques. Here are some questions you might ask a mentor teacher:

1. What strategies do you use to involve all students in answering questions, especially those who are quieter or less confident?
2. How do you handle situations when students struggle to answer a question or provide incorrect answers?
3. Can you provide examples of questions that have worked well in your classroom?
4. How do you adjust your questioning techniques for different age groups or skill levels?
5. What techniques do you use to encourage all students to participate in discussions?

VOICES FROM THE FIELD

The Importance of a Common Vision for Learning

Katrina Stewart

I fundamentally believe that all students deserve great teachers and a great education, in every grade, subject, school, and classroom. As a

(Continued)

(Continued)

teacher, this means that I must maintain a focus on the big picture of student learning and student impact, while working to become increasingly fluent and intentional in what works. To help anchor thinking around these ideas, our district created a one-page instructional framework of best practices called the Common Vision for Learning.

In the center of the framework is the learning target and success criteria, since impactful practices hinge upon those learning trajectories being set appropriately, intentionally, and meaningfully for students. The center clarifies the "what, why, and how" of the learning. Surrounding the center are other elements of effective instruction—modeling, guided instruction, collaborative learning, and independent learning—each with a clearly stated purpose. Formative assessment weaves through all of these elements, providing recursive opportunities for student voice and feedback. This element informs my thinking and next steps in response to student needs. The margins of the framework contain bulleted reminders about intentional teacher and student actions that contribute toward the vision of "high quality educators creating equitable, rigorous learning experiences in every classroom every day."

Together, these components form the building blocks of the high-quality learning experiences that all students deserve. They help students to meaningfully engage in their learning, consolidate their understanding with peers, and solidify their skills with strategic supports from educators. They also allow for students to develop interpersonal and collaborative skills while maintaining the cognitive lift for the learning. As a teacher, these become the building blocks of my lesson plans and unit design.

The purpose statements within each block sharpen my focus on the impact of my actions. When I plan a model, for example, I am reminded that the purpose is not just to provide an example; instead, it is to give students access to my thinking processes as they apply the learning, and to help them avoid common errors. Similarly, I am reminded that guided practice is much more than working with a partner. Rather, it is an opportunity for me to use strategic questions, prompts and cues with students—individually, in pairs, in small groups—to investigate and challenge their thinking processes to ensure they are on the right pathway toward learning and mastery. These purpose statements keep me intentional, ensuring that the focus stays on learning rather than the task.

The Common Vision for Learning has also provided a shared instructional language and facilitated collaborative conversations. I am in a district with many singletons, where many of us do not have grade-level or course-level colleagues to serve as thought partners. Still, we can share ideas about effective tools, processes, and strategies related to learning based on our classroom experiences through the lens of the framework. Across grade levels and content areas, we can discuss intentional teacher moves and student moves, share successes and challenges, and benefit from one another's thinking as we hone our craft.

Of all those who benefit from the Common Vision for Learning, students stand to gain the most. Though we are early in implementing this framework, aligning our instructional practices can provide students with clear, consistent, equitable access to the high-quality learning opportunities that they all deserve. They deserve to know what they are learning, why it matters, and how they can measure success. They deserve daily opportunities to engage with authentic texts. They deserve to learn from expert thinking, and to navigate challenging learning process with others and on their own. They deserve to be well-prepared for whatever is next. And they deserve educators who are intentional and aligned in their practices for maximum impact on learning. Maintaining the vision makes it easier for me as an educator to remember what my role is all about and how I can leverage it for student growth and success.

BRINGING IT ALL TOGETHER

How we teach matters! In many ways the impact of our teaching is more reliant on how we teach rather than what we teach. The instructional practices we highlighted in this chapter were purposefully selected to communicate to you the importance of this. Regardless of what level you teach, what content area is your specialty, or in some cases the grade level you have been "voluntold" to teach, your instructional practices need to be considered, deliberate, and well crafted. This takes time, and practice but ultimately we know that you can do it!

Our hope for this chapter was to provide you with short actionable instructional practices that you could investigate to determine which you may want to consider implementing in your classroom. Many of us think what has the greatest impact on student learning is how much we know about the content we are delivering, when in fact that is not true. What is more important is actually our ability to manage our instructional practices which improve our credibility in the eyes of our students. With this in mind we hope you gleaned some valuable insights into instructional practices that you can implement and track using the tool at the end of this chapter.

IMPLEMENTATION TRACKER

<table>
<tr><td colspan="2">Attempted toolbox tactic:</td></tr>
<tr><td>Successes:</td><td>Roadblocks:</td></tr>
<tr><td colspan="2">What should I change to be more successful next time?</td></tr>
</table>

<table>
<tr><td colspan="2">Attempted toolbox tactic:</td></tr>
<tr><td>Successes:</td><td>Roadblocks:</td></tr>
<tr><td colspan="2">What should I change to be more successful next time?</td></tr>
</table>

Our colleagues in Corwin have done some brilliant work regarding teacher clarity in the classroom as mentioned in Toolkit Tactic 6.3. Please see the QR code that follows for access to even more great content!

https://qrs.ly/kxgdgj7

To read a QR code, you must have a smartphone or tablet with a camera. We recommend that you download a QR code reader app that is made specifically for your phone or tablet brand.

7

ASSESSMENT: THE MEASURE OF EFFECTIVE TEACHING AND LEARNING

Imagine you're planning a road trip without a map or GPS—chances are, you'd end up lost, frustrated, and probably nowhere near your intended destination. In many ways, teaching without solid assessment practices is like setting off on that journey without direction. Assessment is your roadmap, guiding you and your students toward their learning goals, providing crucial feedback along the way, and ensuring that everyone arrives at the destination together.

When we talk about assessment, we're not just referring to tests and quizzes. It's about planning to gather evidence of student learning in a way that informs your teaching and supports your students in their learning journey. Whether it's through formative assessments like quick exit tickets or summative assessments like final projects, your role as a teacher is to continuously collect data on how your students are progressing. This evidence isn't just for you—it's for your students too. When they can see where they are and where they need to go, they become more active participants in their learning. This is where increasing student voice in the assessment process becomes critical.

Imagine a classroom where students have a say in how they demonstrate their learning. Maybe one student chooses to create a video presentation, while another opts for a written report. By offering choices, you're not only honoring diverse learning styles, but you're also fostering a sense of ownership and engagement in the assessment process. When students feel their voices matter, they're more likely to invest in the work they're doing, which in turn leads to deeper learning.

Of course, the purpose of assessment isn't just to collect evidence for the sake of it. It serves a critical function at various stages of the learning process. Initial assessments, or preassessments, are like diagnostic tools. They help you understand where your students are starting from, what prior knowledge they bring to the table, and where there might be gaps. This information is invaluable in guiding your instructional planning. It allows you to tailor your lessons to meet the needs of your students, ensuring that your instruction is targeted and effective.

Then there are postassessments, which come after instruction has taken place. These assessments are your way of checking whether the learning objectives have been met. Did your students grasp the key concepts? Are they able to apply what they've learned in new and meaningful ways? Postassessments give you that feedback, allowing you to reflect on your teaching and make any necessary adjustments moving forward. They also provide students with a clear picture of their progress, helping them understand their strengths and areas for improvement.

But here's the thing about assessments—they're only as useful as the feedback they generate. And this is where staying on top of your grading becomes essential. Timely and constructive feedback is crucial for student growth. It's not just about assigning a grade; it's about providing insights that can guide students in their learning journey. Whether you're grading a stack of essays or reviewing a set of math quizzes, your feedback should be specific, actionable, and geared toward helping students improve.

Now, let's be real—grading can be overwhelming, especially when you have a full class load. But here's a tip: Don't let the pile get too high. Develop a routine that allows you to stay on top of your grading. Maybe it's dedicating a certain amount of time each day to grade a few assignments, or setting aside specific days each week for feedback. Find what works for you and stick to it. Not only will this help you manage your workload, but it will also ensure that your students receive timely feedback that they can act on.

Solid assessment practices are the foundation of effective teaching. By planning to gather evidence, increasing student voice in the assessment process, understanding the purposes of initial and post-assessments, and staying on top of your grading, you're setting the stage for a classroom where both you and your students can thrive. Assessment isn't just a box to check—it's a powerful tool that, when used effectively, can transform your teaching and enhance your students' learning experiences. So, as you continue to build your teaching toolkit, remember this: Assessment is your compass, guiding you and your students on the path to success.

As you embark through the rest of this chapter, we wanted to make sure you had a clear map of the concepts and ideas that will be explored more in depth. As we mentioned previously in the introduction, do not feel pressured to try and apply all of these ideas, rather explore as many of these as you can and apply what piques your interests or needs. Enjoy exploring the following toolbox tactics:

1. Questioning Techniques for Assessment: Using questioning techniques as checks for understanding, and assessments will help us navigate through our lesson to determine where we need to go next with our students.
2. Planning to Gather Evidence and Assessment: As much as possible, we do not want our assessments to happen by accident. By planning to gather evidence, we will be more deliberate in knowing which assessments we will be giving and when.
3. Increasing Student Voice in Assessments: Students know more about their current level of understanding than we give them credit for, thus designing assessments that promote more student voice will enable us to gain a greater understanding of our classroom growth and achievement.
4. Grading to Find Balance: There will be times in the school year where the grading seems to pile up, yet it is important for us to understand the ebb and flow of grading and allow ourselves to find balance.
5. Taking Away Barriers to Student Success: Students come to us with preconceived barriers that we may not have considered. Knowing how to navigate these barriers will allow us to be more impactful with our assessment practices.

TOOLBOX TACTIC 7.1 QUESTIONING TECHNIQUES FOR ASSESSMENT (THE CRAFT OF QUESTIONING)

Case: *New teachers should understand that questioning techniques are a powerful tool for both formative and summative assessment. As a new teacher, mastering questioning techniques is crucial for effective teaching and student learning. The key words (command words) in a question aid the student in understanding how to engage with and respond to the questions. As the teacher you need to ensure the students know what cognitive process the question is asking them to perform. We will examine how questions serve as excellent tools for your assessment of student learning.*

From Tim: *As a kid, I loved to play 20 Questions. Inquiry, wonder, and critical thinking skills for me stemmed from how to ask great questions. As a student, I asked my teachers lots of questions. It was my Grade 6 teacher (and principal) Mr. Hansen who got me hooked on the value and power of great questions. If there were facts or books on the topic, I wanted to read them. If there was a show or documentary, I wanted to watch it. With current events, I wanted to talk about it in class. Mr. Hansen leveraged questions to allow me, the inquiring mind, to do the heavy lifting of thinking more deeply about what I was learning and more so, get me to understand the why behind every subject. Never underestimate the power of a great question!*

In Toolbox Tactic 6.5, we shared a variety of ideas as to how effective questioning techniques can help you keep students engaged and participate to a greater extent in learning conversations. Now, we are going to spend some time looking closely at how the types of questions you use, in terms of determining student understanding, thought processes, and assessing student progression toward mastery, play a crucial role in your assessment practices. We will refer to this as the *craft of questioning*.

THE CRAFT OF QUESTIONING

We know that questioning, especially in how we formulate and pose questions, plays a crucial role in assessing student learning. From check-ins that give us valuable formative feedback, to the questions we ask in our various assessment tasks, it is important as a new teacher to know how to leverage questioning effectively. Review Figure 7.1. In this table, we will detail several ways that asking questions can help inform you in terms of student learning.

7.1 How Questions Inform Our Assessment Practice

Immediate Feedback on Understanding	When teachers ask questions during a lesson, students' responses provide instant feedback on their understanding. Correct or well-thought-out answers indicate comprehension, while incorrect or incomplete answers reveal gaps or misconceptions.
Revealing Thought Processes	By asking students to explain their reasoning or how they arrived at an answer, teachers can assess the depth of their understanding. This helps identify whether students are merely memorizing information or truly grasping the concepts.
Identifying Misconceptions	Effective questioning can uncover common misconceptions that students may have. By addressing these immediately, teachers can prevent misunderstandings from taking root.
Assessing Critical Thinking	Higher-order questions that require analysis, evaluation, or synthesis can reveal how well students are developing critical thinking skills. Responses to such questions show whether students can apply what they've learned to new situations or think creatively about the material.
Monitoring Progress Over Time	By consistently asking questions throughout a unit or course, teachers can track student progress. This ongoing assessment helps teachers adjust their instruction based on how well students are mastering the material.

(Continued)

(Continued)

Differentiating Instruction	Teachers can use questioning to assess the varying levels of student understanding within the class. This information allows for differentiated instruction, where teachers can provide additional support or challenges based on individual student needs.
Encouraging Reflection and Self-Assessment	When students are asked to generate their own questions or reflect on their answers, they engage in self-assessment. This process helps them recognize what they know and where they need to focus their efforts, providing teachers with insight into their metacognitive skills.
Guiding Lesson Pacing	Student responses to questions can help teachers decide whether to move on or revisit a topic. If most students are struggling, it's a sign that more time needs to be spent on that content.
Building Classroom Dynamics	Regular questioning fosters an environment where students feel comfortable expressing their understanding (or lack thereof). This openness allows teachers to more accurately assess the learning environment and address any issues that might be affecting student learning.
Informing Summative Evaluation	In cases where students must write a summative assessment, e.g., a test, exam, final essay, or project, the way teachers craft questions has an impact in determining what students understand, know, and how they can genuinely demonstrate their learning. Careful consideration of question stems and command words is important.

In its truest sense and application, *questioning* is a dynamic tool that not only checks for understanding but also deepens learning, guides instruction, and creates a more interactive and responsive classroom environment.

CRAFTING QUESTIONS

How you create questions in considering the cognitive tasks you are asking students to undertake warrants careful consideration. Let's explore some key ideas about the "command words" we use in questions that will help you create relevant and impactful questions for the learning tasks you create for your students. Keep in mind that we discussed analyzing the learning progressions earlier in Toolbox Tactic 4.2; thus the questions we use in class should follow the same pattern of increasing in complexity. For this, we offer the following seven big ideas:

1. **Clarifying Expectations**
   - Command words set clear expectations for students. For example, words like *describe*, *analyze*, or *compare* guide students on what kind of response is required. This helps students focus their thinking and approach the question in the right way.
2. **Targeting Different Cognitive Levels**
   - Different command words align with different levels of Bloom's taxonomy. For example,
     - ***List*** or ***identify*** targets recall of facts.
     - ***Explain*** or ***summarize*** targets understanding.
     - ***Analyze*** or ***evaluate*** targets higher-order thinking.
   - By carefully selecting command words, teachers can design questions that challenge students at various cognitive levels.
3. **Promoting Critical Thinking**
   - Command words like ***justify***, ***critique***, or ***debate*** encourage students to think critically, support their arguments with evidence, and engage in deeper analysis. This fosters higher-level thinking and discussion.
4. **Ensuring Alignment with Learning Objectives**
   - The command words in your questions should align with your lesson's learning objectives. For example, if the objective is for students to understand a concept, you might use ***explain*** or

describe. If the goal is to apply knowledge, ***demonstrate*** or ***apply*** would be more appropriate.

5. **Differentiating Instruction**
   - By varying command words, teachers can differentiate instruction to meet the needs of diverse learners. Simpler command words can be used for students who need more support, while more complex ones can challenge advanced students.
6. **Encouraging Specificity and Precision**
   - Command words help ensure students give specific and precise answers. For instance, ***outline*** might prompt a brief summary, while ***discuss*** encourages a more detailed exploration of the topic.
7. **Improving Assessment and Feedback**
   - When command words are used consistently, it becomes easier to assess student responses and provide feedback. Teachers can evaluate whether students met the specific demands of the question and give targeted feedback accordingly.

As a new teacher, you will want to be very intentional with choice of command words to ensure that questions are effective in assessing student understanding, guiding thinking processes, and achieving learning objectives. As we discussed in Toolbox Tactic 4.2, the use of Bloom's taxonomy as a tool is a great way to deliberately enhance the use of command words. We have provided you with a graphic (in the Appendix) that you are likely quite familiar with. What we want you to remember is that it is truly the combination of both how (the art) you ask questions and what (the craft) questions you ask that have the greatest benefit to your students.

QUESTIONS TO ASK YOUR MENTOR OR COLLEAGUES

1. How can I design questions that assess both surface-level understanding and deeper critical thinking?
2. How can I effectively use student responses to questions as a formative assessment tool during lessons?
3. How can I use questioning techniques to differentiate assessment for students with varying abilities?

4. What are some effective ways to scaffold questions to build students' confidence and understanding?
5. What are some strategies to use questioning to gauge student understanding in real-time during a lesson?

TOOLBOX TACTIC 7.2 PLANNING TO GATHER EVIDENCE AND ASSESSMENT

Case: *A critical piece of understanding our learner and their learning journey requires us to assess their progress. Often we may wonder where we should be getting assessments from, or when in the year we should be giving assessments. Another operative wonder may be how many assessments do we need, and how many need to be graded. Assessing students can be quite daunting as a new teacher. These feelings and wonderings can be mitigated if we take some time to plan out our assessments.*

From Vince: *When teaching a course for the first time, I often relied on my collaborative team to tell me which assessments we would be assigning to students. This would occasionally lead to a scattered lesson delivery in an attempt to 'cover' everything necessary for the assessment. I found out very quickly that when I was more deliberate in factoring in formative and summative assessments in my planning process it was MUCH easier for me to see growth and progress with my students.*

SCHOOL STORIES

A Smorgasbord of Assessments

It was late August when Carmela Rodriguez received a call to let her know she had been hired to teach in a school district five hours away from her hometown. The school she would be working at, Twin Peaks Middle School, had an influx of new students apply over the summer and she was an emergency hire. This meant she was hired onto the district with less than a week before the start of the school year, giving her very little time to pack her things and start her dream job of being a middle

(Continued)

(Continued)

school science teacher. Luckily for her the school district had apartments to rent, and even assisted her with the move, which allowed her to focus on preparing to teach in a new town as a first year teacher.

The day before the official start of the school year—in this district teachers go back to school a week before the students to prepare for start-up—Carmela received an email from her department chair informing her that he had her back and that he had all of the assessments for her science classes. When meeting him for the first time the next day at the start up meeting, he gave her password access to his cloud drive folder. Upon opening it up, Carmela found over 200 files for each of her classes. This was great! She spent the morning sifting through the drive excitedly, yet as the morning progressed she became increasingly frustrated.

At lunch she sat with the other new teachers, who all shared similar stories. At this school it was commonplace to just use the assessments from the previous year. All four new teachers complained how they were spending too much time trying to determine what files were meant to be assessed when, and more importantly how to assess the students using assignments, quizzes, and tests they had never seen before.

Surely there had to be a better way, but what?

If you found yourself in Ms. Rodriguez's shoes this year, or have a friend who has been through that experience, you are not alone. Generally the people who give us resources are always doing so with the greatest of intentions, but what they tend to forget about is that a drive full of random files is often no better than a file folder full of unorganized papers. It takes too long to sift through the smorgasbord to figure out what is worth using and what is not. Believe us when we say to you, the best assessments are the ones that are purposefully planned with a desired result in mind. Planning for assessment requires us to have clarity about our expectation of student success, a system to gather evidence of learning, and the desire to use that information to have an impact on our own practice.

PLANNING TO GATHER EVIDENCE: DO I EVEN KNOW WHAT I SHOULD BE LOOKING FOR?

We included this question half-jokingly, but the reality is the assessments we give our students should not happen by accident.

We are also using the terms assessment and evidence interchangeably in this section as we do feel that the purpose of our assessments should be to gather evidence about our students and the progress they are making. That is why we need to be deliberate in knowing the purpose of our assessments, the function or type of assessment we are giving, and the link to the standards we are teaching. Have a look at Figure 7.2 below to help understand what we mean by this.

7.2 Planning to Gather Evidence

What is the purpose of this assessment?	If the assessment will be used to make a judgment on the current level of student understanding (like a formative assessment or check for understanding), then it is imperative as the teacher you adjust your instructional practice. This means using the data from the assessment to make changes prior to evaluating for grades.
	If the assessment will be used to make a final evaluation on the students' level of understanding (like a summative assessment for grades), then it is imperative as the teacher you ensure you have already engaged in a few formative assessments first. The first time students are assessed on their understanding should not be for grades.
How will this assessment function for my students?	Will the assessment be standardized for all students? If so, we need to make sure students are familiar with the processes of standardized tests. Some states and provinces have government standardized tests that we need to prepare students for, and many of us do so by giving practice tests. We must make sure students are familiar with the processes before

(Continued)

(Continued)

	assuming they know how to take the assessment.
	Will students have a choice in how to prove their understanding? If so, we need to ensure that all students have an equitable rubric that allows them to prove their understanding in a manner that they see fit all while ensuring the integrity of the assessment itself.
To what extent does this assessment link to the standards or outcomes?	It is imperative to link the assessments you are giving to the students against your local content standards or outcomes. Knowing which standards or outcomes are being addressed in your assessment will help you determine how many assessments are necessary. Hint, it is extremely difficult to hit all of your required content if you are not mapping your assessments, or if you are trying to individually address each standard or outcome with its own assessment. Make sure you are stacking your content outcomes or standards to assess more efficiently.
Where did this assessment come from?	This question may seem a bit obvious, but trust us when we say that not all assessments are created equally. It is imperative that you know the source of your assessment. There are certain degrees of quality when we purchase resources online, or use AI exclusively (without editing). This is also true when we are given resources from colleagues. We must ensure that we know exactly what content our resources are assessing, and while we may not have time to create all of these from scratch we should still engage in due diligence to make sure they are appropriate for our classes.

USING OUR SUCCESS CRITERIA FOR EVIDENCE GATHERING

In Toolbox Tactic 6.3, we discussed the notion of clarity in the classroom, one of the specific aspects of this we discussed were success criteria. (If you have not read that tactic yet, we recommend doing so before continuing with this tactic.) These success criteria statements are a great way to help us plan for specific evidence gathering, particularly when we check for understanding. Checking for understanding is a systematic approach used to monitor and adjust teaching based on student responses. An essential characteristic of assessment and evaluation is the teacher and the student actively and continuously monitoring student learning using specific strategies designed to gather evidence. Checks for understanding can range in complexity, intensity, and the means by which learners make their thinking visible. For example, checks for understanding can be written, verbal, or kinesthetic, depending on the criteria for success. The more directly and quickly you can obtain the necessary evidence, the better. Our success criteria can help us generate an evidence gathering plan as seen in Figure 7.3.

EVIDENCE GATHERING PLAN—PART 1

7.3 Evidence Gathering Plan Template

Success Criteria	Predicted Evidence
This is where we would list our specific success criteria.	This is where we would brainstorm what our students should do to demonstrate learning.
Example Below	**Example Below**
I can predict products for different chemical reactions.	Think-pair-share using demonstrations of each reaction; student questioning during direct instruction using worked examples; guided practice with examples from textbook; exit ticket using clickers

Source: Adapted from Hattie et al. (2020). *Great teaching by design: Moving From Intention to Implementation in the Visible Learning Classroom*. Corwin; Sweeney & Harris. (2017). *Student-Centered Coaching: The Moves*. Corwin.

Once we plan to gather evidence as we exemplified in part 1, the next step is actually doing something with the success criteria! In part 2, we have provided a template of an evidence gathering tool that you can use when you circulate to check for understanding (Figure 7.4). This tool will help you qualitatively gather evidence of student progress and give you a place to house your observations. The ultimate goal of this template is to hopefully align what you are observing in part 2 with what you planned or hoped to see in part 1.

EVIDENCE GATHERING PLAN—PART 2

Evidence Gathering Plan Example

Student Name: *Luca B.*			
Success Criteria	**Observed Doing**	**Heard Saying**	**Saw Writing**
This is where you would place your success criteria.	This is where you would write what you are observing your student doing related to the success criteria.	This is where you would write what you are observing your student saying related to the success criteria.	This is where you would write what you are observing your student writing related to the success criteria.
Example Below			
I can **explain** the process for balancing equations.	*Luca is using scratch paper to practice balancing equations.* *Luca is seeking help from peers.*	*Luca is explaining to his peer that he is struggling to follow the guided instruction.*	*Luca successfully balanced the equation despite verbally admitting he struggled during guided instruction.*

Source: Adapted from Hattie et al. (2020). *Great Teaching by Design: Moving From Intention to Implementation in the Visible Learning Classroom*. Corwin; Sweeney & Harris. (2017). *Student-Centered Coaching: The Moves*. Corwin.

WHAT DO I DO WITH THE DATA?

As mentioned at the beginning of this tactic, it is imperative we do something with the data and observations we are collecting. As such, we wanted to include a few reflection questions for you to consider as you start to analyze your observations, assessments, and data.

1. What does this assessment tell me about the evidence of my impact on student learning?
    a. Through this question we can also solicit specific feedback from students while they are being assessed.
2. What does this assessment tell me about student growth and student achievement?
    a. We almost exclusively focus on achievement as a marker of success, but we encourage you to look at individual student growth as well. Ex. I would rather have a student grow from 40 percent to 50 percent, than a student who stays stagnant at 65 percent.

Use these questions in conversation with your colleagues to help direct your analysis of your assessments, if you are considering other ways you can leverage the data you are collecting, or are planning on collecting consider Ms. Lee's experience below.

VOICES FROM THE FIELD

Using Initial and Post Assessments

Ms. Aitana Lee

El Dorado Elementary School

Last year, my fellow kindergarten teachers and I embarked on teaching a new math curriculum called iReady Classroom Mathematics. This curriculum provided us with a lot of very valuable information and resources to help teach math in the classroom. Two of the very valuable resources within the curriculum were the initial and postassessments that were given to every student before each lesson started and after each lesson finished. I loved this because it measured students' growth over the course of the lesson and demonstrated what students truly learned. In my class, I used the initial assessment as a baseline for the students' learning.

(Continued)

(Continued)

After my students took each initial assessment, I identified areas of need and strengths. I made goals for my students to help them be successful and I made note of areas that I would make sure to address and take my time on during the lesson. The initial assessment was my favorite part about starting a new lesson because I saw what prior knowledge students had and I took that as an opportunity of how I could help strengthen and build their confidence within the particular math topic we were on. After completing the lesson and spending time teaching and practicing, the student took a postassessment.

This is a very important tool because I could compare the results of the postassessment to the initial assessment to see how much students grew and improved over a short period of time. As a teacher it is important to back up student success with data. Without data, words are just an opinion based on how I think my students did during the lesson. Both the initial and postassessment clarify any questions and set in stone what students actually know and have learned. In my experience, even though some students may not have mastered the lesson, using both the initial and postassessment shows individual student growth. You cannot have one without the other, it is critical to students' success to have both the initial and postassessment.

QUESTIONS TO ASK YOUR MENTOR OR COLLEAGUES

1. How do you organize your assessments to ensure as much of the content is being addressed as possible?
2. What might be the best possible course of action to determine what constitutes a high-quality assessment?

TOOLBOX TACTIC 7.3 INCREASING STUDENT VOICE IN ASSESSMENTS

Case: *Our classrooms are complex places that tend to have a wonderful mix of student abilities, and attitudes. This is particularly true when we look at assessments. We know students learn at different paces and often can demonstrate their learning in a variety of ways. The caveat of this notion is that we are only one teacher, and often restrict the ways in which students can share what they know. This is not on purpose;*

rather it is generally due to time, and other constraints. How then, might we encourage more student voices in our assessment practices?

From Wayne: *At the midpoint of my teaching career, I discovered that student voice was a valuable tool in helping me understand what my students were thinking and what they wanted from me. Part of that was learning how my students wanted to be assessed. One particular group challenged me on why I let them choose different novels but only assessed them one way. That really forced me to think and out of that I developed a number of assessments and had the students give me feedback on which ones they liked and which ones they did not. Out of that experience I grew a great deal as a teacher "of all my students."*

PROCESS OVER PRODUCT ASSESSMENT PRACTICES

When you think of the way you were assessed as a student in school, chances are there was a heavy emphasis on the products you were required to submit to prove your understanding. Products are important for students to prove their learning, but should not be the only way we are collecting evidence of learning. There should be a heavy emphasis on process focused assessments as well. Process focused assessments are intended to be markers of student understanding as they are engaging in the learning. Process focused assessments require students to be a part of the assessment process, meaning us as teachers will need to leverage more student voice. Using that voice to determine where we move next in our instruction will be vital to having an impact on student growth and achievement. In the pages that follow you will find three sections: whole-group, student self-assessments, and structured assessments, each section will have some ideas to consider as we attempt to engage more student voice in our process focused assessments.

WHOLE-GROUP ASSESSMENTS

You already know our approach to questioning if you read Toolbox Tactic 7.1, but we wanted to emphasize the importance of whole group evaluation. What we mean by this is an alternative to the standard approach of "Does anyone have a question?" or "Everyone got it?" We have students in our classes who are more introverted, and may not approach answering questions verbally with as much enthusiasm as others. Thus, we thought we would include a couple of ideas for your consideration.

Using whiteboards to solicit answers AND confidence. Many classroom teachers are already using whiteboards in their classroom to get students to answer questions. We want to offer an extension to that idea. Rather than exclusively ask students for an answer, we suggest prefacing with a "confidence indicator." Have students draw a sun if they are clear on how to answer, or a cloud if they are unclear of how to answer or are not confident in providing an answer. Solicit the suns and clouds first, prior to asking for an answer. From an instructional standpoint, if most of the class is cloudy then it does not serve to ask for an answer. This process allows for students to provide insights on whether they are ready to answer a question or not. The image below is a sample of the whiteboard some of us use in our classes.

Source: Sun and cloud icon by Istock.com/etoitosawa; whiteboard image by istock.com/damiangretka

Have students rank their understanding rather than asking for yes or no. When students are asked yes or no questions, they tend to answer yes in a large group so they do not appear like they are unsure. Rather than doing that, you can ask students to rank themselves according to established criteria. The sample rubric shown in Figure 7.5 is what Vince uses when he works with teachers and students alike. The sample is intended to highlight the importance of shared understanding when looking at assessments. Using this table allows students to rank themselves, and understand that attached to each ranking is an action they will be responsible for.

7.5 1-2-3 Ranking

1	2	3
a. Things are unclear. b. I need more information to improve my understanding. c. I have specific questions about the content.	a. Things are somewhat clear. b. A conversation or time to process individually will improve my understanding. c. I have specific wonderings about the content.	a. Things are very clear. b. I can use my understanding to help others with their questions or wonderings. c. I am interested and want to learn more.

STUDENT SELF-ASSESSMENTS

Assessing a classroom of students can be a daunting task especially considering the desire to maintain an understanding of the progress our students are making as individuals. In many ways, we feel that students generally have a great sense of where they are in their learning and we must harness their desire to tell us so. Thus, self-assessments are a great way to encourage students to tell us what they know!

Use success criteria with a ranking scale for students to reflect. Using the same ranking table presented above, we can have students rank their understanding and confidence against the communicated success criteria. The sample template shown in Figure 7.6 provides students opportunities to indicate their level of confidence and understanding. Students will copy down the success criteria and at the end of the lesson can submit this table to you as an exit ticket.

7.6 Success Criteria Ranking Scale Template

Success Criteria Statements	1	2	3
I can . . .	______ ______ ______ ______	______ ______ ______ ______	______ ______ ______ ______

(Continued)

(Continued)

Success Criteria Statements	1	2	3
I can . . .	________ ________ ________ ________	________ ________ ________ ________	________ ________ ________ ________

***Turning* I can *into* Can I?** Another plausible use of success criteria and exit tickets would be to turn the *I can* statements presented at the beginning of class, into *Can I?* reflection statements students should consider. For example, if we look at our sample success criteria statement from Toolbox Tactic 7.2, we could see how students may reflect using this idea. Notice on the table shown in Figure 7.7 we left an open section for a rationale. This is where students would have the opportunity to answer the *Can I?* section and rationalize or prove their response.

Can I? Reflection

I can . . .	Can I . . .?	Rationale
I can **explain** the process for balancing equations.	Can I **explain** the process for balancing equations?	________ ________ ________ ________

STRUCTURED ASSESSMENTS AND GRADING

We know that structured assessments are a necessary part of the assessment process in our classrooms and schools. However, we often find that in the preparation for these types of assessments we often exclude student voice. Part of the reason is due to the structure of these types of assessments, which are mostly multiple choice in nature. We offer the following consideration: Reduce the amount of multiple choice questions and require students to explain or justify their response. You will see a template for this on the next page.

Multiple Choice Answer	Justify Your Response
______________________ ______________________ ______________________ ______________________	______________________ ______________________ ______________________ ______________________
______________________ ______________________ ______________________ ______________________	______________________ ______________________ ______________________ ______________________

I know I am close! Response. Having a justification section for the multiple choice question also opens up an opportunity for your students to explain or justify their response if they are unsure whether they can narrow down their answer to just one choice. Students can use the justification section to explain their reasoning, and we as teachers can use that interpretation to assign grades as well as gain a better understanding of the thought processes that go into structured responses. A reminder for this idea in the classroom, is that you will need to reduce the number of questions on the assessment to allow ample time for students to authentically justify their response.

USING ASSESSMENTS IN CLASS

The ideas presented in this tactic are intended to complement the existing assessment practices occurring in your class. We often find that assessments are where teachers are consistently given lots of advice, resources, and support from colleagues and mentors. So we hope these provide you with some ideas to leverage more student voice in your assessment practices. As we move to the end of this tactic, though, we wanted to provide you with two reminders regarding your assessments in your class.

- When you find one or two practices that work well for you, stick with them. It is very tempting to constantly switch up assessment styles, but remember for every new assessment type our students exert some cognitive load in learning how to complete the task. In this case for our students, predictability can be our friend.

- The ultimate goal of any classroom is to encourage students to work toward the mastery of a standard or objective. This means that as a teacher we should be open to allowing students multiple attempts at assessments to ensure they are learning from their efforts and moving to mastery.

QUESTIONS TO ASK YOUR MENTOR OR COLLEAGUES

1. What types of assessments are we encouraged to use with students as directed from our school leaders or district leaders?
2. How reliant are we on the assessments provided from our curriculum or other resources? To what extent do you deviate away from these to meet the needs of your students?
3. How might you consider leveraging more student voice in your assessment practices?

TOOLBOX TACTIC 7.4 GRADING TO FIND BALANCE

Case: *Every class comes with the responsibility to track progress and communicate that progress to the students, parents, and school. The most common way to communicate progress is through grading and reporting. The crux of grading and reporting tends to be that we often find ourselves in the ebb and flow stages. Sometimes our grading responsibilities are less, and sometimes our grading responsibilities feel like a tidal wave of assessments to grade, and an insurmountable stack of papers to read. How then might we progress through our year to ensure we are grading in a timely manner without burning ourselves out?*

From Tim: *In my first year of teaching, I had too many assignments and worse, I graded them all. I bombarded students with too many miscellaneous surface level quizzes, tests, and essays. I was paddling frantically against the current of assessing everything when I should have been going with the flow of student learning. In time, largely to preserve my well-being and with sage advice from a mentor, I learned* *to better select the learning targets and tasks to assess. I harnessed the power of formative feedback and ensured students had more voice in the process. Balance is important—it just takes a little time to find what is right for you and your learners.*

Finding the right balance between grading (as with many other aspects of your professional life) and your personal world can feel like paddling a canoe down an unfamiliar river. Each stroke requires rhythm and timing to stay on course, as does the careful management of your professional and personal life to avoid the rocks and stay in the current. If you focus too much on one side, you'll find yourself veering off track, unable to move forward effectively getting caught in the branches sticking out from the banks. In this metaphor, your grading is one side of the canoe and your personal life is the other.

Grading is important as it provides feedback for your students, helps you assess their understanding, and guides your future teaching. Just as paddling on one side moves the canoe, you need to carve out time to ensure this work gets done. However, too much focus without balance or a clear understanding on why and what should be marked could leave you mentally drained. If all your energy goes into grading late into the night or on weekends, you'll end up paddling in circles, constantly busy but feeling like you're not making progress in other areas. Remember, you are grading aspects, not all, of the assignments as students cannot take in every piece of feedback. Be specific in what you mark and be clear with students what you are working on with them so they understand why you graded certain aspects and not others. And make sure your grading is leading to discussions with your students. Spending long hours just to create a number for your gradebook does little to help your students take command of their learning, incorporating feedback and becoming better at the skills you are teaching.

On the other side of your canoe is your personal life, which needs equal attention. Taking time for yourself to relax, exercise, or spend time with loved ones is like dipping your paddle into the water to keep your canoe moving in a straight line. Neglecting this side can lead to burnout, stress, and reduced effectiveness in the classroom. If you don't take care of yourself, your energy to invest in your students will diminish. Life, like a river, will have its rapids and calm waters, and during the stressful times, the temptation may be to overcompensate on grading, but resist it. Your canoe needs balance to navigate through both.

So when should you do your grading, and when should you paddle for yourself? Think of it in terms of rhythm. Schedule your grading in manageable chunks, perhaps an hour or two after school, or set aside a specific morning session will help. Avoid long marathon sessions that take away from the rest of your life. Similarly, make sure to schedule personal time, whether it's going for a walk, reading, or spending time with friends. Just as paddling requires a steady, alternating rhythm to move the canoe forward, alternating between work and relaxation helps you maintain balance.

Remember, as with paddling a canoe, efficiency comes from maintaining a steady pace rather than exhausting yourself with too much effort on one side. Stay balanced, and you'll move smoothly through both your teaching responsibilities and personal life.

THE BALANCING ACT OF GRADING

Balancing the professional demands of teaching, such as grading, with maintaining a meaningful personal life is crucial for long-term success and well-being. As grading can easily consume a teacher's free time, it provides a fitting vehicle for understanding how to achieve this balance.

The first step is to set clear boundaries around grading. Rather than letting it spill into every available evening or weekend, schedule specific times for it. For example, dedicate an hour or two each day after school or choose a couple of afternoons during the week to focus solely on grading. This creates a structure that prevents grading from encroaching on your personal life. Additionally, set time limits for grading each batch of papers. Avoid overgrading—providing thoughtful, concise feedback is more valuable than endless comments that could overwhelm both you and your students.

Next, prioritize efficiency. Use tools and strategies that streamline the grading process, such as rubrics or digital assessments that automatically grade certain types of questions. You can also stagger your grading schedule by breaking down large tasks into smaller chunks, such as grading a few papers each day rather than tackling an entire class set in one sitting. This helps prevent burnout and keeps the task manageable.

Most importantly, protect your personal time with the same level of dedication. Just as you schedule time for grading, schedule time for relaxation, hobbies, and socializing. Whether it's spending time with family, exercising, or simply relaxing with a book, these activities are essential for recharging and maintaining your mental health. We spend more time on self-care, and preserving your own health in the next chapter! The key to balance is intentionality. By setting boundaries around grading, working efficiently, and carving out time for yourself, you'll be able to fulfill your professional obligations while still having space for a meaningful personal life.

QUESTIONS TO ASK YOUR MENTOR OR COLLEAGUES

1. How do you manage your time effectively when it comes to grading?
2. How do you decide which assignments need detailed feedback and which can be graded more quickly?

TOOLBOX TACTIC 7.5 TAKING AWAY BARRIERS TO STUDENT SUCCESS

Case: *Students enter our classrooms with many big hopes and dreams, but depending on their circumstances, may have a hurdle on the path to success.*

From Sarah: *I had a student one year; I'll call him M. M had a lot of things going on personally, but made sure I knew that he would NOT be taking part in any written assessments. I, being a cheeky third-year teacher, decided to test this theory and gave him an adapted math test on paper. Well, you'd think I stole his lunch; he was furious with me and showed it. What I came to realize, thanks to my Learning Coach, is that he required differentiation because he has difficulties reading. M was happy to take assessments in class, and was quite good at them, but required differentiation, patience, and understanding. With that, all of his assessments took place with robotics, specifically Dash and Dot robots. He flourished and was so thankful for the accommodation. You're welcome, M; it was the least I could do!*

BARRIERS TO STUDENT SUCCESS

There are many barriers that can impact student success. Oftentimes, they vary depending on different circumstances and environments that are a part of a student's life.

1. **Coursework**: Difficult assignments or homework can cause students to be frustrated with what they are learning in school.
2. **Outside Obligations**: Not all students have the ability to go home and play, eat dinner, and go to bed. More and more, students are heading home after school and have many obligations. Some have part-time jobs; others may have to watch younger siblings. For some students, the expectation is that they prepare dinner or complete household chores. Whatever the reasons, outside obligations can be an exhausting reason for students' success to be compromised. It is important that we are mindful of this.
3. **Mental Health**: For students who may be struggling with mental health issues, the thought of getting out of bed to attend school may be exhausting in itself. Asking a student who is struggling with their mental health to do more can be a huge barrier to their success.
4. **Lack of Resources**: Schools are moving away from textbooks which are dated and may contain outdated information, and leaning on more digital resources like e-publications and STEM-based or project-based learning; however, with education being funded less and less, money must be allocated among the many things a school needs to run. As a result, there may be a lack of resources accessible to students.
5. **Lack of Support Systems**: A student who doesn't have the support of friends, siblings, parents, or other family members may find school and all of its expectations daunting. Students that feel isolated, inadequate, or overwhelmed simply won't put into school what is necessary to be successful.

Overcoming barriers to student success can be complicated, but by helping students implement personal strategies can be helpful. Here are some effective methods to consider as you implement this tactic in your classroom.

EFFECTIVE METHODS

1. **Seek Support**: Allow students the ability to utilize supports like tutors or group study opportunities. Using academic advisors, different types of therapists, and additional resources will help to show students different tools available for their success.

2. **Support Systems**: Connect students from similar regions or that speak the same languages the ability to work with one another. This is incredibly important for students who are newcomers or are learning English as an additional language. Finding cultural groups or centers will help others find connection with people that look like them and, perhaps, know the struggle that immigration can be.
3. **Growth Mindset**: Encourage students to adopt a growth mindset, especially when things are difficult. Instead of allowing comments like "I hate math," coax students to consider saying, instead, "I find math challenging, but I just need a bit of practice."
4. **Success Criteria**: Allow students to cocreate rubrics with you, discussing what success looks like in a specific subject area or on a certain assignment. Model for students how to achieve the success criteria so they can see firsthand how to do their best work.
5. **Self-Care**: Just as adults need to practice self-care, so do students. Brainstorm ways that students can reduce stress and encourage them to try new things that, perhaps, they haven't considered.

Addressing barriers requires all of us to work collaboratively to ensure that students do not fall through the cracks. Inevitably, we won't be able to reach every single individual need, but if we begin to showcase that support, our students will be much better off.

QUESTIONS TO ASK YOUR MENTOR OR COLLEAGUES

1. What can we do to mitigate barriers within our building for our students?
2. How can we help individual students with more complex barriers?

BRINGING IT ALL TOGETHER

Assessment is a necessary entity in teaching; it aids us in seeing what concepts our students may be struggling with, it's an area where we can monitor both student success and areas for growth, and as a road map or GPS to see how far we have come and how far we have left to go. As teachers, we have to prioritize and choose what are the most crucial things to assess—assessing each and every evidence of learning is unnecessary and, quite honestly, defeats the purpose. By working with students to discover what outcomes are necessary to assess and how students will showcase their learning, you will drastically decrease the amount of marking teachers are known to talk about. Additionally, students will take a more serious stance with the things they choose to submit. It's important that we consider the uniqueness of our students and ensure we are approaching assessment with an asset-based lens, meaning we allow our students to use their strengths to prove their learning to us. Assessment should never feel like a punishment, and should always consider the voices and perspectives of our students.

As a new teacher, you may find yourself overwhelmed with the amount of assessment strategies, styles, and approaches used by your colleagues. The intention of this chapter was to assure you that although there is a buffet selection of assessment practices available to you, **what matters most is what you do with the information you gather from your assessments.** An assessment without action or purpose is just an exercise in conformity, so we remind you to assess only what truly matters. As you seek to implement some of the assessment practices highlighted in this chapter we invite you to use the implementation tracker that follows to measure your impact.

IMPLEMENTATION TRACKER

Attempted toolbox tactic:	
Successes:	Roadblocks:
What should I change to be more successful next time?	

Attempted toolbox tactic:	
Successes:	Roadblocks:
What should I change to be more successful next time?	

8

CONCLUSION

You made it! Congratulations, and thank you again for reading through this toolkit. It was our hope that this resource provided insights and ideas for you to consider as you navigate through your first few years of teaching. Perhaps you are reading this as a student teacher or a teacher in an induction program; perhaps you are a newly credentialed teacher or a second-career newly credentialed teacher; or perhaps you are reading this in hopes to find new toolbox tactics to have in your repertoire. Regardless how you found your way to this book, we want you to know that we value the time you spent in these pages as you seek to make a greater impact in your classroom or school. We want to remind you of the goals you set for yourself at the beginning of this book on pg. 18. Spend a few minutes reflecting on your journey and review the extent to which you met your goals.

REFLECTING ON MY GOALS FROM THE BEGINNING OF THE BOOK

Goal #1:
Was this goal met? Was this goal abandoned? Was this goal refined?
Goal #2:
Was this goal met? Was this goal abandoned? Was this goal refined?
Goal #3:
Was this goal met? Was this goal abandoned? Was this goal refined?

So how did you do? Were your goals met, or addressed to the extent you had hoped they would be? If not, there is honestly no stress here. The purpose of this book was to give you actionable ideas and tools to enhance the already stellar job you are doing in the classroom. Although you have reached the end of the book, we are hoping this doesn't mean you will put the book away. You see, it is our hope that this book acts as a resource and a reference for you when you find yourself looking for support and ideas.

We also want to remind you that you are not alone in this teaching adventure! There are countless people who would love to support your journey. Reach out to them. Find your village, consult your mentor, chat with your colleagues, and learn from your students as much as they learn from you. I (Vince) will leave you with a few statements that I use when wrapping up keynote addresses to large groups:

- Never take for granted the impact that you have on your students.
- Your students are lucky to have you and you are lucky to have them.
- Never underestimate the influence you have on someone's day.
- This is a challenging, but rewarding profession but know that ultimately you might be the best part of your students' day.
- Thank you for choosing to make a difference in the lives of your students.

APPENDIX

LOW LEVEL THINKING SKILLS ⟶ ⟵ HIGH LEVEL THINKING SKILLS

Knowledge

Recall / regurgitate facts without understanding. Exhibits previously learned material by recalling facts, terms, basic concepts and answers.

Key words:

Choose
Copy
Define
Duplicate
Find
How
Identify
Label
List
Listen
Locate
Match
Memorize
Name
Observe
Omit
Quote
Read
Recall
Recite
Recognize
Record
Relate
Remember
Repeat
Reproduce
Retell
Select
Show
Spell
State
Tell
Trace
What
When
Where
Which
Who
Why
Write

Actions:

Describing
Finding
Identifying
Listing
Locating
Naming
Recognizing
Retrieving

Outcomes:

Definition
Fact
Label
List
Quiz
Reproduction
Test
Workbook
Worksheet

Questions:

Can you list three ...?
Can you recall ...?
Can you select ...?
How did ______ happen?
How is ...?
How would you describe ...?
How would you explain ...?
How would you show ...?
What is ...?
When did ...?
When did _______ happen?
Where is . . . ?
Which one ...?
Who was ...?
Who were the main . . . ?
Why did ...?

Comprehension

To show understanding finding information from the text. Demonstrating basic understanding of facts and ideas.

Key words:

Ask
Cite
Classify
Compare
Contrast
Demonstrate
Discuss
Estimate
Explain
Express
Extend
Generalize
Give examples
Illustrate
illustrate
Indicate
Infer
Interpret
Match
Observe
Outline
Predict
Purpose
Relate
Rephrase
Report
Restate
Review
Show
Summarize
Translate

Actions:

Classifying
Comparing
Exemplifying
Explaining
Inferring
Interpreting
Paraphrasing
Summarizing

Outcomes:

Collection
Examples
Explanation
Label
List
Outline
Quiz
Show and tell
Summary

Questions:

Can you explain what is happening . . . what is meant . . .?
How would you classify the type of ...?
How would you compare ...?contrast ...?
How would you rephrase the meaning ...?
How would you summarize ...?
What can you say about ...?
What facts or ideas show ...?
What is the main idea of ...?
Which is the best answer ...?
Which statements support ...?
Will you state or interpret in your own words ...?

Application

To use in a new situation. Solving problems by applying acquired knowledge, facts, techniques and rules in a different way.

Key words:

Act
Administer
Apply
Associate
Build
Calculate
Categorize
Choose
Classify
Connect
Construct
Correlation
Demonstrate
Develop
Dramatize
Employ
Experiment with
Group
Identify
Illustrate
Interpret
Interview
Link
Make use of
Manipulate
Model
Organize
Perform
Plan
Practice
Relate
Represent
Select
Show
Simulate
Solve
Summarize
Teach
Transfer
Translate
Use

Actions:

Carrying out
Executing
Implementing
Using

Outcomes:

Demonstration
Diary
Illustrations
Interview
Journal
Performance
Presentation
Sculpture
Simulation

Questions:

How would you use...?
What examples can you find to ...?
How would you solve _______ using what you have learned ...?
How would you organize _______ to show ...?
How would you show your understanding of ...?
What approach would you use to...?
How would you apply what you learned to develop ...?
What other way would you plan to ...?
What would result if ...?
Can you make use of the facts to ...?
What elements would you choose to change ...?
What facts would you select to show ...?
What questions would you ask in an interview with ...?

Bloom's Taxonomy: Teacher Planning Kit

Source: https://www.cebm.net/wp-content/uploads/2016/09/Blooms-Taxonomy-Teacher-Planning-Kit.pdf

Analysis

To examine in detail. Examining and breaking information into parts by identifying motives or causes; making inferences and finding evidence to support generalisations.

Key words:

Analyse
Appraise
Arrange
Assumption
Breakdown
Categorize
Cause and effect
Choose
Classify
Differences
Discover
Discriminate
Dissect
Distinction
Distinguish
Divide
Establish
Examine
Find
Focus
Function
Group
Highlight
In-depth discussion
Inference
Inspect
Investigate
Isolate
List
Motive
Omit
Order
Organize
Point out
Prioritize
Question
Rank
Reason
Relationships
Reorganize
Research
See
Select
Separate
Similar to
Simplify
Survey
Take part in
Test for
Theme
Comparing

Actions:

Attributing
Deconstructing
Integrating
Organizing
Outlining
Structuring

Outcomes:

Abstract
Chart
Checklist
Database
Graph
Mobile
Report
Spread sheet
Survey

Questions:

What are the parts or features of ...?
How is ________ related to ...?
Why do you think ...?
What is the theme ...?
What motive is there ...?
Can you list the parts ...?
What inference can you make ...?
What conclusions can you draw ...?
How would you classify ...?
How would you categorize ...?
Can you identify the difference parts ...?
What evidence can you find ...?
What is the relationship between ...?
Can you make a distinction between ...?
What is the function of ...?
What ideas justify ...?

Synthesis

To change or create into something new. Compiling information together in a different way by combining elements in a new pattern or proposing alternative solutions.

Key words:

Adapt
Add to
Build
Change
Choose
Combine
Compile
Compose
Construct
Convert
Create
Delete
Design
Develop
Devise
Discover
Discuss
Elaborate
Estimate
Experiment
Extend
Formulate
Happen
Hypothesize
Imagine
Improve
Innovate
Integrate
Invent
Make up
Maximize
Minimize
Model
Modify
Original
Originate
Plan
Predict
Produce
Propose
Reframe
Revise
Rewrite
Simplify
Solve
Speculate
Substitute
Suppose
Tabulate
Test
Theorize
Think
Transform
Visualize

Actions:

Constructing
Designing
Devising
Inventing
Making
Planning
Producing

Outcomes:

Advertisement
Film
Media product
New game
Painting
Plan
Project
Song
Story

Questions:

What changes would you make to solve...?
How would you improve ...?
What would happen if...?
Can you elaborate on the reason...?
Can you propose an alternative...?
Can you invent...?
How would you adapt ________ to create a different...?
How could you change (modify) the plot (plan)...?
What could be done to minimize (maximize)...?
What way would you design...?
Suppose you could ________ what would you do...?
How would you test...?
Can you formulate a theory for...?
Can you predict the outcome if...?
How would you estimate the results for...?
What facts can you compile...?
Can you construct a model that would change...?
Can you think of an original way for the ...?

Evaluation

To justify. Presenting and defending opinions by making judgements about information, validity of ideas or quality of work based on a set of criteria.

Key words:

Agree
Appraise
Argue
Assess
Award
Bad
Choose
Compare
Conclude
Consider
Convince
Criteria
Criticize
Debate
Decide
Deduct
Defend
Determine
Disprove
Dispute
Effective
Estimate
Evaluate
Explain
Give reasons
Good
Grade
How do we know?
Importance
Infer
Influence
Interpret
Judge
Justify
Mark
Measure
Opinion
Perceive
Persuade
Prioritize
Prove
Rate
Recommend
Rule on
Select
Support
Test
Useful
Validate
Value
Why

Actions:

Attributing
Checking
Deconstructing
Integrating
Organizing
Outlining
Structuring

Outcomes:

Abstract
Chart
Checklist
Database
Graph
Mobile
Report
Spread sheet
Survey

Questions:

Do you agree with the actions/outcomes...?
What is your opinion of...?
How would you prove/disprove...?
Can you assess the value/importance of...?
Would it be better if...?
Why did they (the character) choose...?
What would you recommend...?
How would you rate the...?
What would you cite to defend the actions...?
How would you evaluate ...?
How could you determine...?
What choice would you have made...?
What would you select...?
How would you prioritize...?
What judgment would you make about...?
Based on what you know, how would you explain...?
What information would you use to support the view...?
How would you justify...?
What data was used to make the conclusion...?

REFERENCES

Berry, A. (2020). Disrupting to driving: Exploring upper primary teachers' perspectives on student engagement. *Teachers and Teaching: Theory and Practice, 26*(2), 145-165. https://doi.org/10.1080/13540602.2020.1757421

Berry, A. (2022). *Reimagining student engagement: From disrupting to driving*. Corwin.

Bishop, R. S. (1990). Mirrors, windows, and sliding glass doors. *Perspectives: Choosing and Using Books for the Classroom, 6*(3), ix-xi.

Black, P., & Wiliam, D. (2018). Developing the theory of formative assessment. *Educational Assessment, Evaluation and Accountability, 30*(1), 5-20.

California Department of Education. (n.d.). *W.2.3 (English Language Arts)*. https://www2.cde.ca.gov/cacs/id/web/5627

Casely-Hayford, J., Lindqvist, P., Björklund, C., Bergström, G., & Kwak, L. (2024). Enculturating a protective professional community: Processes of teacher retention in a Swedish hard-to-staff school. *Education Sciences, 14*(1), 114. https://doi.org/10.3390/educsci14010114

CLANEd. (2024, April 12). *The role of AI in personalized learning*. https://claned.com/the-role-of-ai-in-personalized-learning/#:~:text=Adaptive%20Learning,-Probably%20the%20biggest&text=Platforms%20based%20on%20AI%20can,62%25%20increase%20in%20test%20scores

Corno, L., & Mandinach, E. B. (1983). The role of cognitive engagement in classroom learning and motivation. *Educational Psychologist, 18*(2), 88-108.

Darling-Hammond, L. (2017). Teacher education around the world: What can we learn from international practice? *European Journal of Teacher Education, 40*(3), 291-309.

Darling-Hammond, L., Wei, R. C., Andree, A., Richardson, N., & Orphanos, S. (2009). *Professional learning in the learning profession: A status report on teacher development in the United States and abroad*. National Staff Development Council.

Dreer, B. (2021). Teachers' well-being and job satisfaction: The important role of positive emotions in the workplace. *Educational Studies, 50*(1), 61-77. https://doi.org/10.1080/03055698.2021.1940872

DuFour, R., & Fullan, M. (2013). *Cultures built to last: Systemic PLCs at work*. Solution Tree Press.

Duncan, T. G. (2020). The impact of classroom design on student engagement: A systematic literature review. *Sage Open, 10*(3), 2158244020946345.

Durlak, J. A., Weissberg, R. P., Dymnicki, A. B., Taylor, R. D., & Schellinger, K. B. (2011). The impact of enhancing students' social and emotional learning: A meta-analysis of school-based universal interventions. *Child Development*, *82*(1), 405–432.

Edmondson, A. (1999). Psychological safety and learning behavior in work teams. *Administrative Science Quarterly*, *44*(2), 350–383.

Fendick, F. (1990). *The correlation between teacher clarity of communication and student achievement gain: A meta-analysis*. University of Florida.

Fisher, D., Frey, N., & Hattie, J. (2016). *Visible Learning for literacy, grades K-12: Implementing the practices that work best to accelerate student learning*. Corwin.

Fisher, D., Frey, N., Almarode, J. T., Barbee, K., Amador, O., & Assof, J. (2024). *The teacher clarity playbook, Grades K-12: A hands-on guide to creating learning intentions and success criteria for organized, effective instruction (2nd ed.)*. Corwin.

Fuchs, L. S., Fuchs, D., & Compton, D. L. (2019). Interventions for reading difficulties: A special issue. *Journal of Learning Disabilities*, *52*(1), 3–8.

Fullan, M. (2014). *The principal: Three keys to maximizing impact*. Jossey-Bass.

Gay, G. (2018). *Culturally responsive teaching: Theory, research, and practice*. Teachers College Press.

Harris, J., Grandgenett, N., & Hofer, M. (2010). Testing a TPACK-based technology integration assessment rubric. In *Proceedings of the Society for Information Technology & Teacher Education International Conference* (pp. 3833–3840). Association for the Advancement of Computing in Education (AACE).

Hattie, J. (2009). *Visible learning: A synthesis of over 800 meta-analyses relating to achievement*. Routledge.

Hattie, J. (2023). *Visible learning, the sequel: A synthesis of over 2,100 meta-analyses relating to achievement*. Routledge.

Hattie, J, Bustamante, V, Almarode, J, Fisher, D, & Frey, N. (2020). *Great teaching by design: Moving from intention to implementation in the Visible Learning classroom*. Corwin.

Hattie, J., & Clarke, S. (2018). *Visible learning: Feedback*. Routledge.

Hattie, J., & Donoghue, G. (2016). Learning strategies: A synthesis and conceptual model. *npj Science of Learning*, *1*(1), 1–13. https://doi.org/10.1038/npjscilearn.2016.13

Heritage, M., & Popham, W. J. (2020). *Formative assessment: Making it happen in the classroom*. Corwin.

Johnson, D. W., & Johnson, R. T. (2014). Cooperative learning in 21st century. *Annual Review of Education*, *1*(1), 27–43.

Johnson, D. W., Johnson, R. T., & Holubec, E. J. (2018). *Cooperation in the classroom*. Interaction Book Company.

Kemp, A. H., & Fisher, Z. (2022). Wellbeing, whole health and societal transformation: Theoretical insights and practical applications. *Global Advances in Health and Medicine*, *11*, 1–16. https://journals.sagepub.com/doi/epdf/10.1177/21649561211073077?src=getftr&utm_source=sciencedirect_contenthosting&getft_integrator=sciencedirect_contenthosting

Larrivee, B. (2008). Development of a tool to assess teachers' level of reflective practice. *Reflective Practice*, *9*(3), 341–360.

Little, J. W. (1993). Teachers' professional development in a climate of educational reform. *Educational Evaluation and Policy Analysis*, *15*(2), 129–151.

Luckin, R., Holmes, W., Griffiths, M., & Forcier, L. B. (2016). *Intelligence unleashed: An argument for AI in education*. Pearson Education.

Marzano, R. J. (2017). *The new art and science of teaching: Achieving excellence in every classroom*. Solution Tree Press.

Nalipay, M. J. N., King, R. B., & Cai, Y. (2024). *Happy teachers make happy students:*

The social contagion of well-being from teachers to their students. Springer Science + Business Media, LLC.

Sweeney, D., & Harris, L. S. (2017). *Student-centered coaching. The moves*. Corwin.

Tanner, C. K. (2009). The influence of school architecture on academic achievement. *Journal of Educational Administration*, *47*(4), 453–475.

Tate, M. L. (2015). *Worksheets don't grow dendrites* (3rd ed.). Corwin.

Tate, M. L. (2024). *Engaging the brain: 20 unforgettable strategies for growing dendrites and accelerating learning* (4th ed.). Corwin.

Thomas, A. (2022). *The hate U give*. Balzer + Bray.

Tomlinson, C. A. (2017). *How to differentiate instruction in academically diverse classrooms*. ASCD.

Ware, F. (2006). Warm demander pedagogy: Culturally responsive teaching that supports a culture of achievement for African American students. *Urban Education*, *41*(4), 427–456. https://doi-org.proxy1.lib.uwo.ca/10.1177/0042085906289710

Ware, F. (2025). *Warm demander teachers: Healthy, whole, and transformational*. Corwin.

Williams, K. M. (2022). Exploring new literacies: A case study on technology and teacher development in Cuban primary schools. *The Journal of Media Literacy Education*, *14*(1), 82–93. https://doi.org/10.23860/JMLE-2022-14-1-6

Wong, H. K. (2018). *The first days of school* (5th ed.). Harry K. Wong Publications.

Zhang, L., Chen, J., Li, X., & Zhan, Y. (2024). A scope review of the teacher well-being research between 1968 and 2021. *Asia-Pacific Education Researcher, 33*, 171–186. https://doi.org/10.1007/s40299-023-00717-1

INDEX

CORWIN

To help every educator help every student

We believe that every single student deserves a great education

We believe that knowing our impact is both a privilege and a responsibility

We believe that a fair, stable, and thriving society is built on education

Zeitfracht Medien GmbH
Ferdinand-Jühlke-Straße 7
99095 Erfurt, Deutschland
produktsicherheit@kolibri360.de